A Grammar of Akajeru

GRAMMARS OF WORLD AND MINORITY LANGUAGES

Series Editors
Lily Kahn and Riitta-Liisa Valijärvi

This series consists of accessible yet thorough open-access grammars of world and minority. The volumes are intended for a broad audience, including the scholarly community, students, and the general public. The series is devoted to less commonly taught, regional, minority, and endangered languages. Each volume includes a historical and socio-linguistic introduction to the language followed by sections on phonology, orthography, morphology, syntax, and lexis, as well as additional material, such as text samples. The series aims to promote and support the study, teaching, and, in some cases, revitalisation of languages worldwide.

Lily Kahn is Professor of Hebrew and Jewish Languages at UCL.

Riitta-Liisa Valijärvi is Associate Professor of Finnish and Minority Languages at UCL and Senior Lecturer in Finno-Ugric Languages at Uppsala University, Sweden.

A Grammar of Akajeru

Fragments of a traditional North Andamanese dialect

Raoul Zamponi and Bernard Comrie

First published in 2021 by
UCL Press
University College London
Gower Street
London WC1E 6BT

Available to download free: www.uclpress.co.uk

A CIP catalogue record for this book is available from The British Library.

ISBN: 978-1-80008-095-9 (Hbk.)
ISBN: 978-1-80008-094-2 (Pbk.)
ISBN: 978-1-80008-093-5 (PDF)
DOI: https://doi.org/10.14324/111.9781800080935

Contents

List of tables

Abbreviations and symbols

1, 2, 3	1st, 2nd, 3rd person
ABS	absolutive
adj	adjective
adv	adverb
AKJ	Akajeru
CAUS	causative
COP	copula
DEF	definite (article)
DEM	demonstrative
DIST	distal
DISTPST	distant past
EMPH	emphatic
IMMPST	immediate past
INS	instrumental
INV	invisible
k.o.	kind of
n	noun
NA	North Andaman(ese)
NEG	negative
M	Man (1919–23)
nPST	non-past
part	particle
PGA	Present-day Great Andamanese
PL, pl.	plural
postp	postposition
POSS	possessive
PREV	preverb
PRON, pron	pronoun
PROX	proximal
RB_1	Radcliffe-Brown (1914)
RB_2	Radcliffe-Brown (1933)

REFL	reflexive
sg.	singular
SP	somatic prefix
sp.	species
V	verb
Y/N	polarity question
-	morpheme boundary
=	clitic boundary
[ ]	phonetic notation
~	variant
?	uncertain, unknown
♀	female
♂	male

Preface

The present work is part of our ongoing effort to analyse all the extant material on the now-extinct traditional Great Andamanese languages, as they were documented in the late nineteenth and early twentieth centuries. For a general account of the languages and their documentation, see Comrie and Zamponi (2017).

More specifically, this work provides an analysis, with citation of all original sources, of all the extant material for the Akajeru variety of the North Andamanese language. It also incidentally does the same for the very limited material from the Akabo and Akakhora varieties of North Andamanese, as well as for material documented as not further specified 'North Andaman(ese)'. It does not, however, include the more extensively documented Akachari variety of North Andamanese, to which we plan to devote a separate monograph.

We are grateful to anonymous reviewers for comments on draft manuscripts.

Raoul Zamponi and Bernard Comrie
Macerata, Italy, and Santa Barbara, California, April 2021

1 Introduction

This work is an attempt to describe some aspects of the phonology (Chapter 2), grammatical system (Chapters 3–6) and lexicon (Chapter 8) of Akajeru,[1] a traditional dialect of North Andaman Island – the northern island of Great Andaman in the Andaman Islands – as it was reportedly used around the beginning of the twentieth century. It also aims to offer a complete documentation of Akajeru by supplying, in original transcription and translation, all the material of this dialect from all its known sources, in addition to further unspecified North Andamanese material also recorded in the early 1900s and the scanty material from the two minimally documented traditional North Andamanese varieties Akabo and Akakhora.

Akajeru is agreed to be the main component of Present-day Great Andamanese (PGA) (Basu 1952: 57; Manoharan 1989: 8; Abbi 2006: 22; Avtans 2006: 7; Choudhary 2006: 13; Som 2006: 10), a speech variety remembered in 2013 by five Great Andamanese people in the age range 50 to 58 living on Strait Island who ordinarily speak the Andaman variety of Hindi, only three of whom are today still alive (Abbi 2013: 8; Abbi 2020). Abbi (2013: 14, 26) indicates that, while PGA draws its lexicon from all the dialects of North Andamanese, its grammar is primarily based on Akajeru. She also reports (p. 21) that almost all speakers of PGA claim Akajeru as their mother language (cf. also Manoharan (1989: 8)), the other heritage dialects being marginalised and ignored. In Chapter 7, we will attempt to evaluate the consistency of the Akajeru component in PGA by comparing forms and constructions of the two speech varieties.

In this chapter, we will present the sources that document Akajeru (section 1.1) and some background information about its speakers (section 1.2), as well as attempt to define the type of relationship that links Akajeru to the other speech varieties once spoken on North

Andaman Island as well as to the rest of the Great Andamanese language family (section 1.3).

1.1 Sources

The primary sources for this work are the fragments of Akajeru (words, phrases and some short sentences) contained (*passim*) in the pages of Alfred R. Radcliffe-Brown's monograph *The Andaman Islanders* (1922), which gathers the results of his anthropological research carried out on the Andamans between 1906 and 1908. Although the languages of the archipelago were not the main object of the British anthropologist's activity, this volume contains an appendix titled 'The spelling of Andamanese words' (pp. 495–7) with some observations on the languages of Great Andaman and Little Andaman. This linguistic information was substantially increased in the second edition of the volume (Radcliffe-Brown 1933, hereafter RB_2), in which the above-mentioned appendix is replaced by a separate brief essay on the sounds and the grammar of the Andamanese languages ('The Andamanese languages', pp. 495–504) with some first-hand material on Akajeru and Önge (Little Andaman) and some other data on the Akabea language of the southern portion of Great Andaman from Portman (1898). This chapter, as well as the rest of the monograph, also contains numerous forms and constructions generically presented as 'North Andaman[ese]' (or, in abbreviation, 'NA'; note that except in extended direct quotes, where we preserve the original terminology, we use 'North Andamanese' for the language, 'North Andaman' for the geographic area). Probably, for these forms and constructions there is 'very little difference (...) between the four tribes of the North (*Aka-Čari*, *Aka-Ko̲ra*, *Aka-Bo* and *Aka-J̌eru*)', as Radcliffe-Brown (p. 53) indicates in presenting a set of 11 terms used to denote kinship relationships in North Andaman. Of the 85 words recorded by the anthropologist in RB_2 as 'North Andamanese' and for which (thanks to him) we know the exact Akajeru equivalent form, 83 are also Akajeru forms, the two exceptions being <dula> 'moon' (Akajeru: <čirikli>) and <ali> 'lightning' (Akajeru: <ele>). It is therefore highly probable that at least most of the 'North Andamanese' hapax legomena contained in RB_2 are specifically Akajeru words or words also used in this specific dialect.[2]

Radcliffe-Brown, in 1914, had already published an article dedicated to the languages of the Andaman Islands (hereafter RB_1). This work contains grammatical notes on Önge and some words of Akajeru, a few of which (five) are not included in RB_2. The appendix to Radcliffe-Brown (1922) also includes two expressions not found in RB_2; otherwise, all material in the former is also in the latter, and we refer consistently to page numbers in RB_2.

Another source containing material of the traditional speech of the Akajeru is a dictionary of Akabea by Edward H. Man, Officer in Charge of the Andamanese in 1875–9, first published in 1919–23 as a series of supplements to the journal *Indian Antiquary*.[3] In Appendix VI (pp. 169–72), this dictionary (hereafter M) contains a 'Comparative list of words in certain Andaman dialects as recorded in 1876–79. Words indicating various organs and portions of the human body', including 46 Akajeru ('âkà-yêre') anatomical terms.

The only other Akajeru linguistic material of which we are aware is a list of 28 toponyms published in Temple (1903: 31). These and several other Andamanese toponyms were gathered in situ by Man in the framework of the Census of the Andamanese outside the Penal Settlement undertaken in 1901. We reproduce the list in its entirety here: <Anâto> (Dot Island), <Âr-kōl> (Latouche Island), <Chaka-mit-kòito> (bay W. of Cadell Point), <Chàubalo-râ-chéto> (encampment on S. side of Casuarina Bay), <Chíro-méo> (Snark (? Shark)[4] Island), <Chólop-râ (Wreck Point), <Iltomata> (Brown Point), <Ina-ta-râ-jóle> (encampment at S. W. of Pembroke Bay), <Jíre-míku> (hill on N. side of Saddle Peak), <Karáne-téo> (Kwangtung Island), <Kárate-tàt-chíro> (Casuarina Bay), <Ko-po> (point between Yulik and Lamia Bay), <Lau-tíche> (Camp Bay), <Méo-pong> (territory within a radius of few miles of Cadell Point), <Miriti-râ pong> (Stewart Island), <Pârò> (Eileen Bay), <Pâroto-míku> (Saddle Peak), <Pòròng-chíro> (Austin Strait), <Rengo-to-tía> (south extremity of Lamia Bay), <Tâ-burongo> (north of Cadell Point), <Tàkla> (Aves Island (also Berkeley group)), <Tára-chíro> (Bacon Bay), <Tàu-chàu> (encampment at E. end of Austin Strait), <Tàu-kàt-chíro> (Pembroke Bay), <Tàul-l'âr-míku> (Sound Island), <Tébi-chíro> (N. Reef Island), <Tòrop-tot-chéto> (encampment on N. side of Casuarina Bay), <Yulik> (point North of Tara-lait).

Portman (1898: 11) observes: 'The Andamanese have always been able to explain to me the names of places, even when these names would seem to have some very remote origin'. He also shows (pp. 108–15) that several toponyms of the middle and southern sectors of Great Andaman are transparent compound words or have the structure of noun phrases and include, mostly, common nouns denoting tree species, parts of the tree or the human body and geographical objects.

Table 1.1 Some Akajeru common nouns attested also in toponyms

Toponym component	Akajeru	Akachari	PGA	Meaning
<âr-míku>[a]	*aramiku*	-	*imik^{h}u*[b]	'space under'
<burongo>[c]	*eburɔŋo*	-	*eburɔŋo*	'side of the body'
<lau>	*lau*	*lau*	*lao*	'spirit'
<méo>	*meo*	*meɔ*	*meɔ*	'stone'
<râ pong>[d]	*ɛrapoŋ*	*arapoŋ*	*p^{h}oŋ*	'cave'
<rengo>	*reŋo*	-	*reŋo*	'tree sp.: *Ficus laccifera*'
<tàu>	*tau*	*tau*	*tɔo*	'sky'

Notes

[a] Without somatic prefix *ara-* ~ *ɛra* (3.2.1.2) in <Jíre-míku> and <Pâroto-míku>.

[b] 'space inside' (cf. *ara-mik^{h}u* 'stomach').

[c] Without somatic prefix *e-* in <Tâ-burongo> (3.2.1.3).

[d] Without somatic prefix *ɛra-* ~ *ɛra* in <Méo-pong>.

At least three of the Akajeru toponyms in Temple's list look like compounds or noun phrases.

<Chíro-méo>	<Méo-pong>	<Tôrop-tot-chéto>	
ʧiro-meo	*meo-poŋ*	*torop*	*t=ot-ʧeto*
sea-stone	stone-hole	tree_sp.	DEF=SP-hump (?)

Some of the common nouns or roots we can identify in Temple's toponyms also occur in Radcliffe-Brown or Man's Akajeru linguistic material and have known cognates in Akachari, a dialect of the north of North Andaman (1.3.1), and/or PGA. These are given in Table 1.1.

Other nouns apparently contained in the toponyms were not recorded elsewhere. They are similar or identical in form to Akachari and/or PGA nouns denoting for the most part tree species or animals. These are given in Table 1.2.

1.1.1 Radcliffe-Brown as a linguist

Alfred R. Radcliffe-Brown (1881–1955), our main source for the traditional Akajeru language, spent the years 1906–8 conducting fieldwork in the Andaman Islands, almost immediately after completing his undergraduate studies in Cambridge in 1905.[5] This was his first extensive field project. His publications setting out the results of his work (Radcliffe-Brown 1914,

Table 1.2 Some Akajeru common nouns attested only in toponyms

Akajeru	Akachari	PGA	Meaning
<chíro>	*ʧiro*	*siro*	'sea'
<kòito>	*kɔitɔ*	*koeto ʈɔŋ*	'jackfruit tree: *Artocarpus chaplasha*'
<ko-po>	-	*kɔpo*	'banana tree'
<ot-chéto>	-	*ɔtcɔːʈʈɔ*	'hump'[a]
<pârò>	*paro*	-	'k.o. grub'
<tôrop>	-	*toːrop*	'tree sp.'
<téo>	*teɔ*	*teo*	'iguana, crocodile'[b]

Notes

[a] If <ot-chéto> is the equivalent of the PGA form here indicated, it is possible that it used adjectivally ('humpbacked') in <Tôrop-tot-chéto> (see above).

[b] Cf. also Akajeru <teo> 'bird sp.'.

1922, 1933) contain little explicit reflection on methodology, in particular linguistic methodology, and indeed most of the few remarks on the latter included in Radcliffe-Brown (1922) were not carried across to the second edition of 1933. His interests were clearly primarily (and appropriately) social anthropological, with linguistics very much an auxiliary discipline. He mentions no explicit linguistic training, other than some in phonetics.

His original intention was to work with the Önge on Little Andaman Island, whose language belongs to the Ongan family, quite distinct from the Great Andamanese family to which Akajeru belongs, and at that time virtually undocumented. However, he abandoned this plan when faced with the difficulties of acquiring a new language with no aids.

> I spent nearly three months camped with natives of the Little Andaman, giving most of the time to learning their language ... At the end of three months I found that at the same rate of progress it would take me two or three years to learn to speak the language sufficiently well to begin to question the natives about their customs and beliefs and understand their answers ... (Radcliffe-Brown 1922: vii–viii)

He therefore decided to turn his attention to the Great Andamanese language family, already the subject of documentation by Edward Horace Man and Maurice Vidal Portman (see the References), though concentrating on North Andamanese, the language furthest removed from those on which Man and Portman had worked most intensively, in particular Akabea. He describes the progress of his language skills as follows:

> In my work amongst the natives of the Great Andaman I at first made use of Hindustani, which the younger men and women all speak more or less imperfectly, and gradually acquired a knowledge of the dialects of the North Andaman. (Radcliffe-Brown 1922: viii)

It is impossible to judge from this clearly what level of proficiency he acquired in North Andamanese. An indication of how he viewed the role of language learning in anthropological fieldwork can be gleaned from the following remarks relating to Opuchikwar (from the Middle Andamanese branch of Great Andamanese) and Akarbale (from the South Andamanese branch of Great Andamanese).

> Towards the end of my stay in the islands I was able to obtain the services as interpreter of a man of the Akar-Bale tribe who spoke English well and was of considerable intelligence ... With his help I was able to do some work with the Akar-Bale and A-Pucikwar tribes, and I found that with such an interpreter I was able to obtain much fuller and more reliable results than I could by using my own knowledge of the native language supplemented by Hindustani. If I had had his services from the outset my work would have been much easier and more thorough. (Radcliffe-Brown 1922: viii)

Apparently he was happy to work without having to learn the language if this was possible.

Radcliffe-Brown did, however, indicate his intention to publish further on the indigenous languages of the Andaman Islands:

> The languages of the Andaman Islands are chiefly of interest as affording material for the study of comparative grammar and the psychology of language. I had hoped to be able to make some use of the large mass of linguistic material collected by Mr E. H. Man and arranged by Sir Richard Temple, which the latter was so kind as to permit me to examine. Mr Man, however, expressed the intention of publishing that material himself. Therefore, rather than delay longer, I began the publication of my own linguistic studies in a series of papers in the journal *Anthropos*, of which, however, only the first had appeared when the outbreak of war

> interrupted them.[6] I cannot say when the publication of these notes will be resumed. (Radcliffe-Brown 1922: viii–ix)

However, the three works discussed below are the only relevant ones that he published; the appendix to RB_2 is the only substantial linguistic publication subsequent to the remarks quoted above.

With specific regard to phonetics, we return in Chapter 2 to the consideration of the level of accuracy of Radcliffe-Brown's transcriptions, for now we note his own recognition of his limitations:

> My knowledge of the principles of phonetics when I went to the Andamans was very inadequate, and my subsequent studies have shown me that my phonetic analysis of the Andamanese languages is far from satisfactory. Further I have consciously omitted to distinguish in writing between different sounds nearly related to each other, such as different forms of the consonants *t*, *d*, *k* and *g*. (RB_1: 37)

> Although I had acquired some knowledge of phonetics before I went to the Andamans, as a necessary part of the preliminary training of an ethnologist, yet it was not really sufficient to enable me to deal in a thoroughly scientific manner with the problems of Andamanese phonetics, and my further studies of the subject give me reason to believe that my phonetic analysis of the Andaman languages was not as thorough as it might have been. (Radcliffe-Brown 1922: 496, fn. 1)

The further studies referred to in this passage took place in the absence of native speakers, so there was no further possibility of checking data directly. After 1908 Radcliffe-Brown did not, as far as we have been able to ascertain, return to the Andamans or have any contact with native speakers of the indigenous languages.

It is easy to be critical in retrospect. We note that Radcliffe-Brown was a trailblazer of social anthropological methodology, and that without his linguistic material we would know virtually nothing of the traditional Akajeru language. We are very much in his debt.

1.2 The Akajeru

When the British, in 1858, established a permanent settlement and penal colony at Port Blair, on South Andaman Island, the Akajeru inhabited the southern portion of North Andaman Island and the northern extremity of Middle Andaman (Portman 1899: 21), their neighbours being the Akabo on the north-west, the Akakhora on the north-east and the Akakede on the south (on Middle Andaman). We do not know how many Akajeru there were at the time of the contact. For the year 1858, the number of the people of the four native groups of North Andaman (Akajeru, Akabo, Akakhora and Akachari) is estimated by Radcliffe-Brown (RB_2: 18) to be about 1,500, based on what the Andamanese were able to tell him of the conditions under which they formerly lived. Between 1901 and 1931, four enumerations of the indigenous populations of Great Andaman were attempted in connection with the census of India (Temple 1903: 6; Lowis 1912: 76; Lowis 1923: 12; Bonington 1932: 22–3). Such enumerations were of course very difficult and liable to error. Limited to the Akajeru and the other three groups of North Andaman, their results are given in Table 1.3.

The demographic decline of the Akajeru highlighted by Table 1.3 forms part of a general demographic collapse of the indigenous populations of Great Andaman after the British established the permanent settlement and penal colony at Port Blair. It is estimated that the indigenous population of the islands, excluding the Jarawa (a group speaking a language unrelated to any other language of Great Andaman),[7] amounted to 3,500 people in the early part of the nineteenth century (Local Gazetteer 1908: 5). Imported diseases (pneumonia in 1868, syphilis in 1876, measles in 1877 and influenza in 1892), to which the islanders had no immunity, decimated the tribes at the end of the nineteenth century. In 1901, only 625 Great Andamanese were left, excluding again the Jarawa (Temple 1903: 6), and subsequent censuses report steadily declining numbers: 455 in 1911, 209 in 1921, 90 in 1931 (Lowis 1912: 76; Lowis 1923: 12; Bonington 1932: 22–3). In 1951, the number of the Great Andamanese had shrunk to about 23. Their number dwindled to an all-time low of only 19 in 1961 (Chattopadhyay 2003: 77; Mohanty 2006: 37). In 1970, the few surviving Great Andamanese, mostly from North Andaman or of North Andaman descent, were

Table 1.3 The demographic decline of the Akajeru

Year	Akajeru	Akachari	Akakhora	Akabo	Total
1901	218	39	96	48	401
1911	180	36	71	62	349
1921	101	17	48	18	184
1931	46	9	24	6	85

relocated on the small Strait Island, off the east coast of Middle Andaman, in an attempt to protect them from diseases and other threats. They were 23 in all (Chattopadhyay 2003: 61). The number of Great Andamanese has slowly increased since then, to 27 (1981), 28 (1989), 32 (1991), 40 (1994), 42 (2001), 50 (2005) and 56 (2013) (Chattopadhyay 2003: 77; Raha 2005: 23; Abbi 2006: 6; Abbi 2013: 19–20). However, the people identified as Great Andamanese since 1970 have included people with partly Burmese or Indian descent.

1.3 Genealogical position of Akajeru and co-dialects

Although Akajeru is regarded as an independent language both in the literature on the Andamanese languages and, usually, in catalogues of the languages of the world (and also has an ISO 639–3 code, like most of the known natural languages: [akj]), in fact, it is one of the four dialects (or, probably, groups of dialects) that were once spoken on North Andaman Island. We have proposed the name North Andamanese for this language (Comrie and Zamponi 2017: 57). The other three (main) dialects of this language (also with an ISO 639–3 code) are the varieties of the remaining traditional groups of the island: Akachari [aci] (1.3.1), Akabo [akm] (1.3.2) and Akakhora [ack] (1.3.3). Together with the extinct Akakede language [akx], once spoken on the northern half of Middle Andaman and on Interview Island (Portman 1899: 21), North Andamanese forms one of the three (well-defined) subgroups of the Great Andamanese language family, the other subgroups, also now extinct, being Middle Andamanese (including the closely related Opuchikwar [apq], Okol [aky] and Okojuwoi [okj]) and South Andamanese (including Akabea [abj] and Akarbale [acl]) (Comrie and Zamponi 2019).

1.3.1 Akachari

At the time of contact, the Akachari inhabited the coast of the northern half of North Andaman and the adjacent small islands (Portman 1899: 21; Temple 1903: 31). Their dialect is the best attested among those traditionally spoken in North Andaman, having been documented, together with Akabea, Opuchikwar, Akakede and Önge, in the *Manual of the Andamanese Languages* compiled by Maurice V. Portman, comprising a comparative vocabulary covering over a thousand headwords and a phrase-book of 100 pages (Portman 1887).[8]

In order to have an idea of the degree of differentiation that separated the traditional forms of Akajeru and Akachari, in Table 1.4 we present a comparative word list of basic vocabulary of the two varieties based on Swadesh's 200-word list as published in Gudschinsky (1956). It must be noted that there are, however, actually only 53 entries in this comparative word list due to the fact that for 144 entries of Swadesh's list no available source indicates the Akajeru and/or the Akachari equivalent. It should also be also taken into account that the Akajeru and Akachari forms of Table 1.4 are given in a tentative, semi-phonetic transcription (see section 2.4, as regards Akajeru).[9]

Table 1.4 Comparative Akajeru–Akachari word list

	English	Akajeru	Akachari	Cognate	Notes
1.	at	*=il*	*=il ~ =l*	+	locative postposition
2.	bad	*etʃai*	*ebekedeŋ*	–	
3.	belly	*itpet*	*pet*	+	Akajeru *itpet* is probably a possessed form (see 3.2.3)
4.	big	*ɛrkuro*	*erkuro*	+	
5.	blood	*tei*	*ete*	+	
6.	bone	*tɔi*	*tɔi*	+	
7.	child	*ottire*	*ottire*	+	possessed form (see 3.2.1.6)
8.	cold	*otʤulu*	*otʤulu*	+	of weather
9.	to die	*e-m-pil*	*e-m-pil*	+	
10.	dog	*bibi*	*bibi*	+	post-contact term
11.	ear	*ɛrbuo*	*erbuo*	+	
12.	eye	*ɛrulu*	*erulu*	+	
13.	to fall	*boto*	*boto*	+	
14.	father	*akamai*	*akamai*	+	
15.	foot	*oŋmatɔ*	*omatɔ*	+	
16.	fruit	*ottʃo*	*ottʃu*	+	
17.	good	*enol*	*nɔ*	+	
18.	hair	*otbetʃ*	*otbetʃ*	+	see endnote 5 to Chapter 7

(Continued table 1.4)

(Continued table 4)

	English	Akajeru	Akachari	Cognate	Notes
19.	hand	*oŋkɔra*	*oŋkɔra*	+	
20.	head	*ɛrʧo*	*erʧo*	+	
21.	husband	*ebui*	*etaru*	–	Akachari *etaru* also = 'man'
22.	I	*tio*	*tio*	+	emphatic
23.	in	*=il*	*=il ~ =l*	+	locative postposition
24.	leaf	*teʧ*	*teʧ*	+	see endnote 5 to Chapter 7
25.	long	*elobuŋ*	*elobuŋ*	+	
26.	man	*etaru*	*etaru*	+	adult male
27.	many	*ʧope*	*ʧope*	+	
28.	meat	*etomo*	*etomo*	+	
29.	mother	*akamimi*	*akamimi*	+	
30.	mouth	*akapoŋ*	*akapoŋ*	+	
31.	neck	*otloŋo*	*otloŋo*	+	
32.	night	*bat*	*bat*	+	
33.	nose	*ɛrkɔto*	*erkɔto*	+	
34.	not	*pu*	*pu*	+	
35.	rain	*ʤiʧɛr*	*ʤoʧɛr*	+	
36.	rope	*luremo*	*luremo*	+	
37.	to say	*akarka*	*eremer*	–	
38.	sea	*ʧiro*	*ʧiro*	+	
39.	to sing	*ʤobi eur*	*ʤobi eur*	+	= 'to sing a song'
40.	sky	*tau*	*tau*	+	
41.	to sleep	*beno*	*beno*	+	
42.	small	*eleo*	*lau*	+	
43.	snake	*ʧubi*	*ʧubi*	+	
44.	star	*kataɲ*	*katain*	+	small star
45.	stone	*meo*	*meɔ*	+	
46.	sun	*diu*	*diu*	+	
47.	there	*kulel*	*kulol*	+	
48.	they	*nio*	*nio*	+	emphatic

(Continued table 1.4)

(Continued table 1.4)

	English	Akajeru	Akachari	Cognate	Notes
49.	this	*kidi*	*kidi*	+	
50.	thou	*ŋio*	*ŋio*	+	emphatic
51.	tongue	*akatat*	*akatat*	+	
52.	tooth	*ɛrpile*	*erpile*	+	
53.	water	*ino*	*ino*	+	
54.	we	*mio*	*mio*	+	emphatic
55.	who	*atʃiu*	*atʃu*	+	
56.	wife	*ebui*	*ebuku*	–	Akachari *ebuku* also = 'woman'
57.	wind	*bɔto*	*bɔto*	+	
58.	woman	*ebuku*	*ebuku*	+	

We may count 54 cognates among the 58 items above, giving a cognation of 93 per cent, which strongly suggests two dialects of the same language, not two distinct languages.

1.3.2 Akabo

The Akabo were located in the central-eastern sector of North Andaman (cf. map II after p. 510 in RB_2). The available documentation of their (traditional) dialect is much poorer than those of Akachari and Akajeru. All that remains is some words transmitted to us by RB_2: the 18 items reported in Table 1.5 (where they are compared with their Akajeru, Akachari and PGA equivalents, when known) and a few proper names: the autonym *akabo* (in <t'a-Bo> 'I am Aka-Bo'; p. 24, with the alternant *a-* of somatic prefix *aka-* ~ *a-* used after a proclitic personal pronoun), the names of three creeks (<Kelera>, <Teradikili> and <Teraut>; pp. 28, 192), the name of a village (<Čaičue>; RB_2: 29) and the names of two supernatural beings (<Biliku> (♀) and <Tarai> (♂); pp. 147, 150) also occurring, with the same form, in Akajeru and Akakhora.

In addition, six words occur in RB_2 (p. 199) that the author probably gathered from an Akabo informant. Four of them are bird names (<čelene>, <čereo>, <čoto̱t> and <to̱ro̱i>). The remaining words are a toponym (<Poroket>) and the name of a male supernatural being (<Pe̱rǰido>). The four bird names and the name of the supernatural being were also recorded by Radcliffe-Brown, with exactly the same form, from Akajeru informants. The toponym corresponds to the PGA noun *pʰoroke̦t*

Table 1.5 Akabo words from RB_2 compared with their equivalents in Akajeru, Akachari and PGA

Akabo	Meaning	Page(s)	Akajeru	Akachari	PGA
<bari>	'fish sp.'[a]	97	-	-	-
<bol>	'fish sp.'[a]	97	*bol*	-	*bol*
<bo̲to>	'wind'[b]	147	*bɔto*	*bɔto*	*bɔtɔ*[c]
<buliu>	'creek'	28	*buliu*	*buliu*	*buliu*
<burto>	'fish sp.'[a]	97	-	*burto*	*bu:rtʰo*
<čiro>[d]	'liver (of an animal)'	103	*ʧiro*	-	*ciro*
<čubi>[e]	'snake'	97	*ʧubi*	*ʧubi*	*ʃubi*
<kibir>	'tree sp.'	103	-	-	*ki:bir*
<ǰutpu>	'alone' (?)[f]	192	*ʤutpu*	-	-
<koloko>[g]	'COLLECTIVE'[h]	28	*koloko*	-	*kɔlɔko*
<ko̲t>	'nest of the white ants'	192	*kɔt*	-	*kɔt̪ot̪co*[i]
<kuato>	'fish sp.'[a]	97	-	-	-
<ńyuri>	'fish sp.: *Plotosus* sp.'	97, 103	*ɲuri*	-	*ɲure*[j]
<or-čubi>	'snake sp.: *Ophiophagus elaps*'	97	*ɔrʧubi*	*orʧubi*	*orʃubi*
<t'>[k]	'I'	24	*t=*	*t=*	*t=*
<tare>	'plant sp.'	103	*tare*	-	-
<ra>[d]	'pig'	103	*ra*	*ra*	*ra*
<uluku>[e]	'snake sp.'	97	-	-	*ulukʰu*

Notes

[a] A fish found in inland creeks.

[b] Also in <Biliku boto> 'N. E. Wind' (lit. 'Biliku wind') and <Tarai boto> 'S. W. Wind' (lit. 'Tarai wind') (RB_2: 147).

[c] 'storm'.

[d] In <ra-čiro> 'plant sp.' (lit. 'liver of pig').

[e] In <uluku-čubi> 'snake sp.'.

[f] This is (also) the name of the first man on earth (RB_2: 383).

[g] Also in the following names of Akabo local groups: <Kelera buliu koloko>, <Teradikili buliu koloko> and <Turaut buliu koloko> (RB_2: 28).

[h] Used with human nouns.

[i] 'mound of white ants'.

[j] 'eel, mangur fish'.

[k] In <t'a-Bo> 'I am Aka-Bo'.

'heaven' recorded by Abbi (2012: 130). The name of the supernatural being (son of <Biliku> and <Tarai>) recalls the PGA name of the first man of the Andaman Islands: *pʰertaɟid̪o* (Abbi 2013: 279).

As Table 1.5 shows, there are no distinctive elements in the poor available lexical material of Akabo that separate this speech from Akajeru. This fact and Radcliffe-Brown's observation that '[a] man of the *Aka-J̌eru* tribe could understand without any great difficulty a man speaking *Aka-Bo*' (RB$_2$: 25) allow us to establish that the traditional varieties of the Akajeru and the Akabo were undoubtedly mutually intelligible dialects of the same language.[10]

1.3.3 Akakhora

The Akakhora occupied the central-western sector of North Andaman (cf. again map II after p. 510 in RB$_2$). The surviving material of their traditional dialect is also minimal. RB$_2$ (pp. 147 and 199) contains the seven common nouns given in Table 1.6, one toponym (<Čaroŋa>) and the names of two supernatural beings (<Biliku> (♀) and <Tarai> (♂)) also recorded from Akajeru and Akabo speakers.

Temple (1903: 31) supplies a list of 11 toponyms: <Bôl-pòli> (inland encampment between Port Cornwallis and Temple Sound), <Cho-â-póng> (Trilby Island), <Kòi-cho> (Pocock Island), <Kôto-par> (Cadell Bay), <Pâro-júe> (Cape Price), <Po-chumbo> or <Bo-pung> (Ross Island at mouth of Port Cornwallis), <Ròth> (Craggy Island),

Table 1.6 Akakhora words from RB$_2$ compared with their equivalents in Akajeru, Akachari and PGA

Akakhora	Gloss	Akajeru	Akachari	PGA
<bo̲to>	'wind'[a]	*bɔto*	*bɔto*	*bɔtɔ*[b]
<kelil>	'bird sp.'	-	-	-
<lo̲ito>	'k.o. root'	*lɔito*	*loito*	*loitok*[c]
<meo>[d]	'stone'	*meo*	*meɔ*	*meɔ*
<mikulu>	'k.o. root'	*mikulu*	*mikulu*	*mikulu*
<peč>	'pot'[d]	*peʧ*	*paiʧ*	*pec* ~ *pʰɛc*
<to̲ro̲i>	'bird sp.'	-	-	-

Notes

[a] Also in <Biliku boto> 'N. E. Wind' (lit. 'Biliku wind') and <Tarai boto> 'S. W. Wind' (lit. 'Tarai wind') (RB$_2$: 147).

[b] 'storm'.

[c] 'k.o. of vegetarian food'.

[d] In <Peč-meo>, a place-name.

<Tàu-râ-míku> (Excelsior Island), <Tébi-chíro> (Chatham Island (Port Cornwallis)), <Tí-kô-dung> (encampment on N. E. of N. Andaman near Reef Island), <Tôlubu-tòng> (Port Cornwallis). In one of these toponyms we can recognise a noun phrase composed of a noun and an adjective.

<Tí-kô-dung>
ti *koduŋ*
place small
'small place'[11]

Another toponym has the structure of a possessive noun phrase, but lacks the expected definite article *t=* (see section 4.1.3).[12]

<Tàu-râ-míku>
tau *(a)ra-miku*
sky SP-space_under
'space under (the) sky'

Overall, we have identified nine Akakhora common words (in one case just the root of a word) in the 11 toponyms published by Temple. None of them was also recorded by Radcliffe-Brown. These forms are given in Table 1.7 together with Akajeru, Akachari and PGA forms with identical or similar shapes.

Table 1.7 Some Akakhora words attested only in toponyms

Akakhora	Akajeru	Akachari	PGA	Meaning
<râ-míku>	*aramiku*	-	$imik^hu$[a]	'space under'
<bôl>	-[b]	*bol*[c]	*bol*	'tree sp.: *Hibiscus tiliaceus*'[d]
<chíro>	*ʧiro*	*ʧiro*	*siro*	'sea'
<kodung>	-	-	*kod̪uŋ*	'small'
<pâro>	-	*paro*	-	'fish sp.'
<póng>[e]	*erapoŋ*	*arapoŋ*	p^h*oŋ*	'cave'
<tàu>	*tau*	*tau*	*t̪ɔo*	'sky'
<ti>	*ti*	*ti*	$t̪^hi$	'place'
<tòng>	-	*aka-toŋ*	*t̪ɔŋ*	'tree'

Notes
[a] 'space inside' (cf. *ara-mik*^{h}*u* 'stomach').
[b] Cf. Radcliffe-Brown's 'North Andamanese' *bol* '*Hibiscus tiliaceus*' (RB$_2$: 118).
[c] Recorded as '*Melochia velutina*', but probably '*Hibiscus tiliaceus*', like the 'North Andamanese' and PGA forms.
[d] Or, alternatively, 'fish sp.' (Akajeru <bol>, PGA *bol*).
[e] Without somatic prefix *ara-* ~ *ɛra* (3.2.1.2) in <Cho-â-póng>.

The sparse Akakhora material that has reached us also does not contain recognisable unique elements not found in Akajeru. Therefore, it is very likely that what we are dealing with is a further variety of a single language once spoken across the whole North Andaman Island.

Notes

1 A.k.a. Jeru and Jero. In Akajeru, *ʤeru* is the name of a tree of the *Sterculia* genus. In the traditional autonym of the Akajeru, which is also a glottonym, the noun *ʤeru* is prefixed by a reflex of the Proto-Great Andamanese somatic prefix (see section 3.2.1) *aka- 'mouth', in the sense of 'language', like the names of all the other groups of Great Andaman, excluding the Jarawa (see Comrie and Zamponi 2017: 67, n. 8). It is probable that the common occurrence in the Andamanese linguistic and anthropological literature of names of Great Andamanese groups without the somatic prefix 'mouth, language' (like Jeru/Jero or, also, for example, Bo and Bea) follows Richard C. Temple's (1903: 48) decision to discard this prefix, '[f]or the sake of brevity', and use 'the roots only of tribal names' (but note also the earlier terms Puchikwár (for *o-puʧik-war*) and Kol (for *o-kɔl*) in Portman (1896: 362)).

2 In this work, we will also use the 'North Andamanese' linguistic material in RB_2. Forms and constructions recorded by Radcliffe-Brown only as 'North Andamanese' will be reported in this work followed by the abbreviation NA.

3 Also issued in book form as a single volume (Man 1923).

4 The variant names are from the original.

5 His family name at birth was Brown, legally changed to Radcliffe-Brown in 1926. We follow scholarly tradition in referring to him consistently as Radcliffe-Brown.

6 The reference is to RB_1.

7 This language is related to the language of the Önge of Little Andaman Island, with which it forms the Ongan family. The language of the (practically) uncontacted inhabitants of North Sentinel Island could be a third member of this small family.

8 A handful of Akachari words are also contained in RB_2 (pp. 96, 141, 147, 201 and 202).

9 Unlike Radcliffe-Brown, Portman does not distinguish the close-mid front vowel [e] from the open-mid from vowel [ɛ] in his transcription of Akachari and other Great Andamanese languages, although there is a phonemic contrast between them in these languages. The symbol *e* of the Akachari forms of Table 1.1, all from Portman (1887), is therefore a common notation of the two vowels of the mid-front area.

10 Abbi (2012: xxiv) reports that many of the words a woman who came from the Akabo group (Boa Sr) used were not comprehensible to the other speakers or rememberers of PGA. This, of course, does not imply that her speech was totally unintelligible to the other speakers or rememberers of PGA.

11 Cf. *ʈʰikoɖuŋpʰubi* 'big place' in Abbi (2012: 391), analysable as *ʈʰi koɖuŋ pʰu=bi* (place big neg=cop) 'It is not a small place'.

12 The exact same item is also recorded by Temple (1903: 31) as the local name of an island (West Island) in Akachari territory. An almost identical item, with the expected definite article *t=*, is the local name of an island in Akakede territory (Interview Island): <Tàu-tara-míku> (Temple 1903: 32).

2
Phonology

2.1 Phonemes

2.1.1 Consonants

The spelling used by Radcliffe-Brown for transcribing Akajeru and the other North Andamanese dialects makes use of a phonetic transcription, albeit simplified, based on the Anthropos alphabet of Wilhelm Schmidt (1907). He employs 14 consonantal graphemes: <b, č, d, ǰ, k, l, m, n, ń, ŋ, p, r, t, y> (see RB_2: 494). The Akajeru words recorded by Man are written using the following graphemes and digraphs: <b, ch, d, j, k, l, m, n, ng, p, r, t, th>. Of the sound values of four graphemes used by Radcliffe-Brown we have a short description.

> The sign *ŋ* is used for the nasalised guttural or velar stop [*sic*] and *ń* for palatalised *n*;[1] the sounds denoted by *č* and *ǰ*, while varying somewhat in different dialects, frequently approximate more nearly to palatalised *t* and *d* than to affricates *ʧ* and *ʤ*. (RB_2: 496)

There are no words with the palatal nasal [ɲ] among those recorded by Man. The velar nasal [ŋ] is transcribed by the British officer with <ng>, while for [ʧ] ~ [c] and [ʤ] ~ [ɟ] the digraph <ch> and letter <j> are used. Also note that the alternation of *ʧ* and *ʤ* between palatal affricate and palatal stop to which Radcliffe-Brown refers has also been reported for PGA (Basu 1952: 61; Abbi 2013: 51).

Radcliffe-Brown also indicates that in Andamanese languages 'there are variations in the pronunciation of the dental stops *t* and *d*, prepalatal, dental or alveolar, and cerebral enunciation being heard, but it is not evident that these variations constitute distinct phonemes in any of the languages' (RB_2: 496). Retroflection is an areal trait of the Andaman

Table 2.1 Probable Akajeru/NA words with dental and retroflex stops and their orthographic representation

Akajeru/NA		PGA	Meaning
Radcliffe-Brown	**Man**		
<mite>	-	*mitɛ*	'bird sp.'
<otone> (NA)	-	*otoni*	'son-in-law, daughter-in-law'
-	<îr-tap>	*ertap*	'lower jaw'
<taka>	-	*ʈaka*	'bird sp.'
<milite> (NA)	-	*biliʈe*	'mist'
<boto>	-	*boʈo*	'fall'
<e̱ra-bat>	-	*eraːbaʈ*	'tail (of snake or turtle)'
-	<âkà-tât>	*akaʈaʈ*	'tongue'
-	<îr-kît>	*erxiːʈ*	'arm'
<tiriń>	-	*t^{h}iriŋ*	'kingfisher sp.'
<e-tomo>	-	*et^{h}omo*	'flesh, meat'
<ti>	-	*ʈ^{h}i*	'place'
<ti-miku> (NA)	-	*ʈ^{h}imik^{h}u*	'forest, jungle'
<eʈ^{h}aru> (NA)	-	*ʈ^{h}aro*	'man, male' (PGA: 'male')
-	<îr-kâto>	*erkɔʈ^{h}o*	'nose'
<kidi>	-	*k^{h}idi*	'this'
<deko>	-	*ɖek^{h}o*	'enough'
<bido>	-	*biɖo*	'palm sp.: *Calamus tigrinus*'

Islands attested both in Great Andamanese and in Ongan (see Zamponi and Comrie 2020: 31). PGA has three retroflex stops, [ʈ], [ʈ^h] and [ɖ], in phonemic opposition with their dental counterparts [t], [t^h] and [d]. Surely traditional Akajeru had the same three retroflex stops as PGA, but both Radcliffe-Brown and Man fail to recognise them in their transcription of Akajeru or 'North Andamanese' (NA) words (see Table 2.1).

Nor does Radcliffe-Brown's transcription of Akajeru distinguish the aspirated stops [p^h], [t^h] and [k^h] occurring in PGA (Abbi 2013: 50–1) from their plain counterparts. Man's transcription distinguishes [t^h] from [t] by using the digraph <th> for the former and the grapheme <t> for the latter, but neither [p^h] from [p] nor [k^h] from [k] (see Table 2.2).

Table 2.2 Orthographic representation of probable words with [p], [p^{h}], [t^{h}], [k] and [k^{h}]

Akajeru		PGA	Meaning
Radcliffe-Brown	Man		
<ropuč>	-	*rɔpuc*	'one who has lost a brother or sister'
<čop>	-	*cɔp*	'tree sp.'
-	<îr-tap>	*ertap*	'lower jaw'
<po̲ro̲to>	-	*p^{h}ɔrɔto*	'palm sp.: *Caryota mitis*'
-	<ê-pilu>	*ep^{h}ilu*	'abdominal walls'[a]
-	<ông-pông>	*oŋp^{h}oŋ*	'armpit'
<e-tire>	-	*t^{h}ire*	'child'
<Tarai>	-	*t^{h}arae*	'a male supernatural being'
<tiriń>	-	*t^{h}iriŋ*	'kingfisher sp.'
-	<era-thômo>	*arat^{h}omo*	'buttocks'
<ko̲lo>	-	*kɔlɔ*	'sea-eagle'[b]
<ko̲ro>	-	*kɔrɔ*	'shredded palm-leaf fibre'[c]
<mikulu>	-	*mikulu*	'k.o. root'
<kule-l>	-	*k^{h}ulol*	'there (distant)'
<čokoro>	-	*cɔk^{h}ɔro*	'plant sp.'
-	<îr-nôko>	*ɛrnɔk^{h}o*	'cheek'

Notes
[a] PGA: 'belly'.
[b] PGA: 'kite'.
[c] PGA: 'green cane leaf'.

No word explicitly attributed to Akajeru was recorded using the letter <w>, but two 'North Andamanese' forms written with this grapheme can be seen in RB$_2$: <biwu> 'k.o. resin' (also occurring in the compound <biwumɔiʧ> 'torch of resin') and <ewur> 'sing'. In both forms, <w> occurs between two vowel graphemes, the second of which is <u>. This suggests that the letter <w> may represent an epenthetic [w]-glide inserted in two-vowel sequences of the type *Vu* (cf. Abbi (2013: 41, 44–5) for a parallel with PGA).[2] Similarly, it is possible that the <y> of the Akajeru noun <keyip> 'k.o. red pigment', also recorded by

Radcliffe-Brown, is the transcription of an epenthetic glide [y] that surfaces in a a two-vowel sequence of the type *Vi* (cf. Akachari <kéip> ‘id.’; Portman (1887: 213)).

A tentative chart of Akajeru consonantal phonemes, based on the following minimal and, mainly, semi-minimal pairs, is given in Table 2.3.[3] Note that we use *y* for IPA /j/ in this work.

p : b	*petʃ*	‘pot’	*betʃ*	‘hair’
t : ʈ	*mite*	‘bird sp.’	*miliʈe* (NA)	‘mist’
t : tʰ	*otone*	‘son-in-law, daughter-in-law’	*etʰomo*	‘flesh, meat’
t : ʈʰ	*pʰɔrɔto*	‘palm sp.: *Caryota mitis*’	*ɛrkɔʈʰo*	‘nose’
tʰ : ʈʰ	*tʰiriɲ*	‘kingfisher sp.’	*ʈʰi*	‘place’
ʈ : ʈʰ	*ʈaka*	‘bird sp.’	*eʈʰaru* (NA)	‘man, male’
ʈ : ɖ	*boʈo* (NA)	‘fall’	*biɖo* (NA)	‘palm sp.: *Calamus tigrinus*’
k : kʰ	*mikulu*	‘k.o. root’	*ʈʰimikʰu* (NA)	‘forest’
tʃ : dʒ	*tʃoː* (NA)	‘plant sp.’	*dʒo*	‘eating, food’
tʃ : y	*akatʃari* (NA)	‘Akachari’	*maya*	‘sir, mister’
m : n	*mio*	‘we’	*nio*	‘they’
n : ɲ	*tʃelene* (NA)	‘bird sp.’	*beɲe*	‘bird sp.’
n : ŋ	*nio*	‘they’	*ŋio*	‘you’ (sg.)
ɲ : y	*reɲa* (NA)	‘possessions’	*maya*	‘sir, mister’
r : l	*kɔro*	‘shredded palm-leaf fibre’	*kɔlo*	‘sea-eagle’

2.1.2 Vowels

There are seven vowel graphemes used by Radcliffe-Brown for transcribing Akajeru: <a, e, e̲, i, o, o̲, u>.[4] ‘The sign e̲ is used for the open *e* (ɛ) and o̲ for the open *o* (ɔ)’ (RB_2: 496). We presume that the remaining five graphemes have their approximate IPA value. The vowel graphemes used by Man are fourteen: <a, à, â, ä, e, ê, i, î, o, ò, ō, ô, u, û>. The graphemes <a>, <à>, <ä>, <e>, <i>, <o>, <ò> and <u> represent short vowels: [ʌ] or [ə], [a], [æ], [ɛ], [i], [ɔ], [o] and [u] (Man 1919–1923: 3). The graphemes <â>, <ê>, <î>, <ō>, <ô> and <û> represent long vowels: [ɑː], [eː], [iː], [ɔː], [oː] and [uː] (Man 1919–1923: 3). While, on the one hand, Radcliffe-Brown distinguishes two mid front vowels

Table 2.3 Consonant phonemes in Akajeru

		Labial	Dental	Alveolar	Retroflex	Palatal	Velar
Stops	**Voiceless unaspirated**	p	t		ʈ		k
	Voiceless aspirated	p^{h}	t^{h}		$ʈ^{h}$		k^{h}
	Voiced	b	d		ɖ		
Affricates	**Voiceless**					ʧ	
	Voiced					ʤ	
Nasals	**Voiced**	m		n		ɲ	ŋ
Rhotics	**Voiced**			r			
Laterals	**Voiced**			l			
Glides	**Voiced**					y	

Table 2.4 Probable Akajeru/NA words with long vowels and their orthographic representation

Radcliffe-Brown	**Man**	**PGA**	**Meaning**
<čo> (NA)	-	*co:*	'plant sp.'
<e̱ra-bat>	-	*era:baʈ*	'tail (of snake or turtle)'
<roa>	-	*ro:ɔ*	'canoe'
<talar> (NA)	-	*ʈa:lar*	'k.o. stone'
<terkobito> (NA)	-	*tɛrkobito:*	'centipede'
<oŋ-ko̱ra>	<òng-kōra>	*k^{h}o:ra*	'hand, finger'
-	<îr-kît>	*erxi:ʈ*	'arm'
-	<òng-mâ-tō>	*oma:ʈʈɔ*	'foot'
-	<òm-rap>	*onrɛ:p*	'spine'

([e] and [ɛ]), but does not note vowel length, on the other hand Man does not distinguish the two mid front vowels, but does mark vowel length (at least in most cases; see Table 2.4).

Table 2.5 gives a plausible chart of Akajeru vowel phonemes, based on the following minimal and semi-minimal pairs and keeping in mind that vowel length is phonemically contrastive in PGA (Abbi 2013: 39–40)

Table 2.5 Vowel phonemes in Akajeru

	Front	Central	Back
Close	i iː		u uː
Close-mid	e eː		o oː
Open-mid	ɛ ɛː		ɔ ɔː
Open		a aː	

(as well as in other Great Andamanese languages; see Zamponi and Comrie 2020: 50 for Akabea), even if vowel length can only be recovered for a handful of items in the documentation of Akajeru/North Andamanese.

i : e	*ino*	'water'	*enol*	'good'
e : ɛ	*ʧereo*	'bird sp.'	*ʤiʧɛr* (NA)	'rain' (n)
ɛ : a	*ɛraːbaʈ*	'tail (of snake or turtle)'	*arabela* (NA)	'younger person of the same generation'
a : ɔ	*maya*	'sir, mister'	*mɔyo*	'tree sp.: *Sterculia* sp.'
ɔ : o	*bɔto*	'wind'	*boto*	'fall' (v)
o : u	*ʧop*	'tree sp.'	*ʧup*	'k.o. basket'

2.2 Stress

Stress is not marked by either Radcliffe-Brown or Man. In none of the languages of the Great Andamanese family (including PGA) is it phonemically relevant. Non-phonemic stress, in all the languages, falls on the initial syllable of the root, at least ordinarily.

2.3 Syllable structure

The maximal syllable structure in Akajeru is CCVVC (where VV indicates a diphthong).

(1)	(C_2)	(C_1)	V_1	(V_2)	(C_3)	Example	
			V_1			**o**.*lo*	'adze'
			V_1		C_3	**ot**.*bo*	'back'
			V_1	V_2		*ʧu*.**ei**	'plant sp.'
			V_1	V_2	C_3	**air**	'foam on a rough sea'
		C_1	V_1	V_2		**tɔi**	'bone'

	C_1	V_1	V_2	C_3	*kɔ.***rɔin**	'tree sp.: *Dipterocarpus laevis*'
	C_1	V_1			***ra***	'pig'
	C_1	V_1		C_3	***pir***	'palm sp.: *Calamus* sp.'
C_2	C_1	V_1			*oŋ.***brɔ***.no*	'ankle'[5]

Consonant clusters are, in general, rather infrequent morpheme-internally, although they readily arise at morpheme boundaries (see, for example, *ot-ʧo* 'head', *oŋ-p*^{h}*oŋ* 'armpit' and *ɛr-boa* 'lip' in section 8.1).

2.4 Our transcription of Akajeru

In the rest of this work, we use for Akajeru (and Radcliffe-Brown's North Andamanese) a tentative semi-phonemic transcription in which – given that aspiration and retroflex consonants are not recognised orthographically and vowel length is not noted in the most important source of this dialect (from which most of the following examples were drawn), viz. RB$_2$ – the IPA symbol *p* may also represent p^h, *t* may also represent t^h, *ʈ* and $ʈ^h$, while *d* may also represent *ɖ* and vowel symbols may represent short or long vowels. We emphasise that this is the best that can be done reliably given the phonetic limitations of the available documentation. Grafting values from PGA onto Akajeru is impossible in cases where we do not know the PGA equivalent, and would be irresponsible in cases where we do, since PGA is not simply the linear descendant of Akajeru (see Chapter 7) and there is no guarantee that such values would be correct.

Notes

1 Occasionally, <ny> is also used for palatal nasal *ɲ* by Radcliffe-Brown, as in <ara-nyu> 'village', <benye> 'bird sp.' and <čainyo> 'plant sp.'.

2 Various other words were however transcribed by Radcliffe-Brown as if they contain a vowel sequence *Vu* without an intervening [w], e.g. <lau> 'spirit', <tau> 'sky', <diu> 'sun' and <ačiu> 'who'. Probably, speakers of traditional Akajeru did not insert the epenthetic [w]-glide in *Vu* vowel sequences consistently, just like the speakers or rememberers of PGA (Abbi 2013: 41).

3 No minimal nor semi-minimal pair is available in the material at our disposal for the contrasts *p* vs. p^h, *t* vs. *d* and *d* vs. *ɖ*, but cf. Abbi (2013: 50–1) for evidence for a phonemic opposition between these sounds in PGA.

4 A further grapheme, <a̲>, is used by Radcliffe-Brown for transcribing the name of a kind of bucket: <ta̲r> (RB$_2$: 497, 498). This grapheme, said to denote a 'back *a* as in Southern English "father"' (RB$_2$: 497), i.e. the open back [ɑː], in this specific term would seem rather to represent the open-mid back vowel [ɔː], as suggested by the transcriptions of the Akachari word for the same kind of bucket in Portman (1887): <tár> (p. 207), <tāūr> (p. 155) and <tāūrāū> [*sic*] (p. 137) (<āū> being the representation of the sound of '*aw* in *awful*'; Portman 1887: 1).

5 The only example we have for syllable-initial CC is the word *oŋ.brɔ.no* 'ankle' (or possibly *om.brɔ.no*; see 3.2.1.5 and the entry *oŋbrɔno* in section 8.1) recorded by Man. However, both Abbi and Manoharan give PGA equivalent forms without the *b* (see again the entry *oŋbrɔno* in 8.1), so the example is questionable. Perhaps *b* is a purely phonetic epenthetic sound here, although another form recorded by Man and containing, just like *oŋbrɔno*, the derivational prefix *oŋ-* ~ *om-* (3.2.1.5) and a root beginning in *r* does not show any trace of *b*: *omrap* 'spine' (see the corresponding entry in section 8.1). Consonant clusters in the onset position are reported as rare by Abbi (2013: 57, 58) for PGA and limited to *tr* and *kʰr*. If phonemic syllable-initial consonant clusters were also possible in traditional Akajeru, we must conclude that no unequivocal evidence of them exists in the scarce material of this dialect that was recorded.

3
Stems

The morphology of Akajeru is agglutinating, like that of all other Great Andamanese languages, and includes prefixes and suffixes, although words rarely contain more than a few morphemes. Prefixes and suffixes are mostly monosyllabic, a few prefixes being disyllabic. Roots are mostly di- or trisyllabic.

3.1 Roots

Most roots have a morphologically and syntactically invariable word class. Many of the roots that were recorded by Radcliffe-Brown can be found without further affixation in the word class of nouns and in derivatives involving somatic prefixes (see 3.2.1) that have the same word class.

(2)	*tei*	'blood'
	e-tei (NA)	'fever'
	ɛra-tei	'menstruation'
	ot-tei	'headache'

(3)	*tomo*	'flesh' (also: 'wood')
	e-tomo	'flesh of the body, meat'
	ɛra-tomo	'buttocks'

A root that appears as a multicategorial lexical base is shown in (4). This root can function both nominally (4*a*), adjectivally (4*b*) and also verbally (61).

(4)	a.	*kimil*	'a brief period of unsettled weather at the end of the rainy season'
		aka-kimil (NA)	'condition of a boy or girl who is passing through the initiation ceremonies'

b. *ɛr-kimil* (NA) 'hot'
ot-kimil (NA) 'hot' (also: 'be hot')

As in other Great Andamanese languages (see Zamponi and Comrie 2020: 73–7 as regards Akabea), some roots have an etymological doublet with a relatable meaning. Examples (5) and (6) show two cases of this.

(5) *ot-ʤumu* (NA) 'dream' (n/v)
ot-ʤumulo (NA) 'shadow; reflection; double of the speaker'

(6) *reŋo* 'tree sp.: *Ficus laccifera*'
reŋko (NA) 'green pigeon'[1]

The following example shows a further possible pair of etymological doublets. Probably, the noun 'sky' has a plain retroflex stop [ʈ], as in PGA (*ʈao* ~ *ʈɔo* ~ *ʈɔ:*), while the verb 'be cold' has perhaps an aspirated retroflex stop [ʈʰ], like the PGA noun *ʈʰɔo* 'cold, winter' (Abbi 2012: 393).

(7) *tau* 'sky'
ot-tau (NA) 'be cold'

There are also four separate roots which seem to share the same historical source in the Akajeru material recorded by Radcliffe-Brown.

(8) *arai-ʧulu* 'after'
tarai-ʧulik 'afterwards'
arai-ʧulute 'younger person of the same generation'
arai-ʧulutu 'follow'

3.2 Affixation

Like all other Great Andamanese languages, Akajeru is rich in derivational morphology. Its attested derivational affixes include 10 prefixes and just two suffixes. Of the attested derivational prefixes, those here termed 'somatic prefixes' are particularly productive, being present in about one third of the ca. 320 words of traditional Akajeru/North Andamanese that were recorded by Radcliffe-Brown and Man.

3.2.1 Somatic prefixes

Somatic (body-part) prefixes are a group of six bound morphemes with the following core meanings:

aka- ~ a-	'mouth'
ara- ~ arai- ~ ɛra-	'abdomen, back'
e-	'body'
ɛr-	'face, arms'
oŋ- ~ om-	'hands, feet'
ot-	'head'

They can be seen attached to nouns, as in (9*a*), adjectives, as in (9*b*), verbs, as in (9*c*) and also to one adverb (9*d*).

(9) a. *aka-poŋ* 'mouth'
e-ŋet 'navel'
ɛr-kɔto 'nose'
oŋ-kɔra 'hand'
b. *e-leo* (NA) 'small'
e-nol 'good'
ɛr-kimil (NA) 'hot'
ot-ʤulu (NA) 'cold'
c. *aka-ʧe* (NA) 'accompany'
arai-ʧulutu 'follow'
ɛra-lio (NA) 'finish'
ot-tau (NA) 'be cold'
d. *arai-ʧulu* 'after'

There is a tendential correlation between semantic content and the co-occurrence of these prefixes with nouns. Nominal roots denoting body parts occur nearly exclusively with a somatic prefix attached. The rare exceptions include a few roots that denote anatomical parts that are not localised to a specific body area (10) and the term *it-pet* 'belly' (possessed form, perhaps), the latter consisting of a root, *pet*, probably also used verbally (cf. PGA *pɛt̪* 'swell'; Abbi (2012: 379)), and a non-somatic prefix whose value or function is unclear (see 3.2.3).

(10) a. *beʧ* 'hair'
ɛr-beʧ 'head hair'
b. *tɔi* 'bone'
oŋ-tɔi 'wrist'

Nominal roots belonging to the following semantic types, as a rule, are not used with somatic prefixes: flora, fauna, celestial bodies, environment, artefacts. The only nominal roots of the semantic types flora and environment also occurring with a somatic prefix in the material at our disposal are given in (11) together with their derivatives including a somatic prefix. The derivatives, it will be noted, belong to different semantic types from the bare nominal roots.

(11)	a.	*ʤeru*	'tree sp.: *Sterculia* sp.'
		aka-ʤeru	'Akajeru'
	b.	*meo*	'stone'
		ɛra-meo	'anchor'
	c.	*odu*	'k.o. clay'
		aka-odu (NA)	'mourner'
	d.	*ʧari* (NA)	'salt water'
		aka-ʧari (NA)	'Akachari'

Nominal roots belonging to the remaining semantic types, that is not referring to body parts and flora, fauna, celestial bodies, environment, artefacts, are morphologically heterogeneous. They can (i) always occur in combination with a somatic prefix (for example, *e-tire* 'child, offspring of an animal'), (ii) occur as a separate word without any other morpheme (for example, *ʤo* 'song') or (iii) occur with or without a somatic prefix (12).

(12)	a.	*mai*	'sir, mister'
		aka-mai	'father'
	b.	*mimi*	'lady'
		aka-mimi	'mother'

Although somatic prefixes have anatomical core meaning, they also have extended meanings, as well as uses that have become lexicalised to the point of opacity. In the range of extended meaning, somatic prefixes exhibit both intra-field and trans-field extensions, that is semantic changes belonging to the same field of anatomy (for example, *ɛr-* 'face' > 'head') or involving changes in meaning to different fields (for example, *aka-* ~ *a-* 'mouth' > 'speech').

In the following subsections, we will attempt to explore the (complex) semantics of each of the six somatic prefixes of traditional Akajeru based on the scanty data at our disposal.

3.2.1.1 aka- ~ a-

The prefix *aka-* ~ *a-* refers to the mouth.

(13)	*aka-poŋ*	'mouth'
	aka-tat	'tongue'

By anatomical contiguity, it also refers to the throat.

(14) *aka-nɔro* 'throat'

Two trans-field extensions of the prefix are documented.

(i) 'mouth' > 'speech'

(15) *akarka* |aka-arka| 'tell, say'
aka-ʤeru 'Akajeru' (language and people) (*ʤeru* 'tree sp.; *Sterculia* sp.')

(ii) 'mouth' > 'eating'

(16) *aka-op* 'boy or girl under certain ritual restrictions chiefly concerned with food'
aka-odu (NA) 'mourner' (*odu* 'k.o. clay')
aka-kimil (NA) 'condition of a boy or girl who is passing through the initiation ceremonies' (*kimil* 'boy or girl during the turtle-eating ceremony')

In the following examples, the prefix expresses meanings different from those indicated above based on unclear semantic extensions.

(17) *aka-mimi* 'mother'
aka-mai 'father'
aka-ʧe (NA) 'accompany'

The allomorph *a-* of this prefix occurs after an overt possessive prefix (18, 67, 98) or a proclitic personal pronoun (58, 60), while *aka-* occurs elsewhere.

(18) *t-a-mimi* 'my mother'
ŋ-a-mai 'your father'

3.2.1.2 ara- ~ arai- ~ ɛra-

Prototypically, this somatic prefix appears to refer to two contiguous, but distinct, parts of the human body: the abdomen, including genital area and its emissions (19), and the back (20).

(19) *ara-ket* 'urine'
ɛra-tei 'menstruation' (*tei* 'blood')

(20) *ɛra-tomo* 'buttocks' (*tomo* 'flesh')

By extension, it also refers to the tail of a snake or turtle.

(21) *ɛra-bat* 'tail (of snake or turtle)'

In addition, some trans-field extensions from the two core somatic meanings can be observed.

(i) 'abdomen' > 'person' (*pars pro toto*)

(22) *ara-litʃu* (NA) 'younger person of the same generation'
arai-tʃulute 'younger person of the same generation'

(ii) 'abdomen' > 'interior'

(23) *ɛra-poŋ* 'cave' (cf. *aka-poŋ* 'mouth')

(iii) 'back' > 'rear part'

(24) *arai-tʃulu* 'after' (adv)
arai-tʃulutu 'follow'

The latter semantic path probably continues further as follows:

(iv) 'rear part' > 'end, termination'

(25) *ɛra-lio* (NA) 'finish'

The Akachari and PGA equivalents of this prefix also occur in the term for 'leg': Akachari <árá chág> (Portman 1887: 44), PGA *ara:buccow* (Manoharan 1997: 463).[2] The Akajeru term for 'leg' was not recorded, but the following trans-field extension of *ara-* ~ *arai-* ~ *ɛra-* (alongside the aforementioned Akachari and PGA forms) suggests that it also had this prefix and that a third body part covered by the prefix was that of the lower limbs.

(v) 'legs' > 'space under'

(26) *ara-miku* 'space under' (cf. *ɛr-miku* 'face')
ɛra-meo 'anchor' (*meo* 'stone')

Other (unclear) values of the prefix, apparently not relatable to any of those indicated above, can be seen in the following stems.

(27) *ara-ɲu* (NA) 'village'[3]
ɛra-lobuŋ 'long, tall'
ɛra-tire 'young shoot of a plant' (cf. *e-tire* 'child, offspring of an animal')

We are not able to find motivation for the choice of one allomorph of the prefix over the other two based on the available data.

3.2.1.3 e-

The prefix *e-* refers to the human body in its entirety.

(28) *e-burɔŋo* 'side of the body'
e-tomo 'flesh of the body, meat'
e-tei (NA) 'fever' (*tei* 'blood')

It is, however, also a sort of 'residue' member of the set of somatic prefixes given its presence in terms for body parts outside the domains covered by the other somatic prefixes.

(29) *e-ŋet* 'navel'
e-pilu 'abdominal walls'
e-ʧɔ 'lap, thigh'

In the following nouns, *e-* refers to the physical person.

(30) *e-taru* (NA) 'man, male'
e-buku (NA) 'woman'
e-tire 'child, offspring of an animal'
e-bui 'husband, wife' (also verb: 'marry, be married')
e-pota-ʧiu (NA) 'father-in-law'

In the following adjectives, the prefix appears to be desemanticised.

(31) *e-leo* (NA) 'small'
e-lobuŋ 'long, tall' (of a canoe, a tree, etc.)
e-nol 'good'
e-ʧai 'bad'

Example (32) shows a verb with *e-*. Here again, it is difficult to identify the semantic content of the somatic prefix.

(32) *e-ur* (NA) 'sing'

3.2.1.4 ɛr-

The prefix *ɛr-* refers to two distinct, noncontiguous parts of the body: the face (including the ears) (33) and the arms (including the shoulder) (34).

(33)	*ɛr-miku*	'face; forehead'
	ɛr-buo	'ear'
	ɛr-ulu	'eye'
	ɛr-kɔto	'nose'
	ɛr-noko	'cheek'
	ɛr-boa	'lip'
	ɛr-pile	'tooth'
	ɛr-tap	'lower jaw'

(34)	*ɛr-kit*	'arm'
	ɛr-bala	'forearm'
	ɛr-kum	'shoulder'

In the following two nouns, the prefix refers to the entire head, overlapping with *ot-*.

(35)	*ɛr-betʃ*	'head hair'
	ɛr-tʃo	'head, skull' (cf. *ot-tʃo* 'head, fruit')

In the following forms, the semantic contribution of *ɛr-* is unclear.

(36)	*ɛr-tʃar*	'heart (seat of affections)'
	ɛr-kuro (NA)	'big'
	ɛr-kimil (NA)	'hot'

3.2.1.5 oŋ- ~ om-

The prefix *oŋ- ~ om-* refers to the extremities: hands and feet.

(37)	*oŋ-kɔra*	'hand; finger'
	oŋ-matɔ	'foot'
	oŋ-kɔtra	'palm of the hand; sole of the foot'
	oŋ-kara	'nail (of finger or toe)'
	oŋ-kudʒu	'knuckle'
	oŋ-tɔi	'wrist'
	oŋ-brɔno	'ankle'

It sometimes also refers to the entire arm.

(38) *oŋ-ba* 'fleshy portion of the forearm'
oŋ-poŋ 'armpit'

In the following example, it refers to the spine.

(39) *om-rap* 'spine'

Man transcribes this prefix as <ông-> and <òng->, except before the rhotic *r*. In this case, we find <òm->: <òm-rap> 'spine'.[4] Probably, the alternant *om-* of the prefix also occurs before a labial consonant, as in Akachari and PGA, although Man (1919–23: 169, 170) recorded the Akajeru term for 'armpit' as <ông-pông>[5] and that for 'foot' as <òng-mâ-tō>.[6]

3.2.1.6 ot-

The prefix *ot-* refers to the head.

(40) *ot-tʃo* 'head, fruit' (cf. *ɛr-tʃo* 'head, skull')
ot-tei 'headache' (*tei* 'blood')
ot-betʃ (NA) 'head hair' (*betʃ* 'hair')
ot-loŋo 'neck'

An extended meaning is 'person' (*pars pro toto*). This is the meaning the prefix has in the possessed form of some terms denoting people. In the case of the word for 'child' (41), the prefix *ot-* replaces the somatic prefix *e-* of its non-possessed form.[7]

(41) *bora* ***e****-tire* (NA) 'Bora (♂) the child'
*bora Ø-****ot****-tire* (NA) 'the child of Bora (♂)'

In other cases, *ot-* appears added to the prefix of the non-possessed form of a term denoting a person.

(42) *Ø-****ot****-ara-bela* (NA) 'his/her younger person of the same generation' (cf. PGA *ara-belo* 'younger sister')
*Ø-****ot****-arai-tʃulute* 'his/her younger brother' (cf. PGA *ara-sulut^{h}uo* 'younger sibling')
*ŋ-****ot****-a-mai Ø-****ot****-arai-tʃulute* (NA) 'your father's younger brother' (but cf. *ŋ-a-mai* 'your father')
*Ø-****ot****-e-bui Ø-****ot****-arai-tʃulute* (NA) 'his wife's younger brother' (but cf. *Ø-e-bui*, also *Ø-ot-e-bui*, 'his wife, her husband')
*Ø-****ot****-ot-one* (NA) 'his/her son-in-law' (cf. PGA *ot-oni* 'id.')

The semantic difference between the two forms in (43) is obscure.[8]

(43)	*Ø-e-bui* (NA)	'his wife, her husband'
	*Ø-***ot***-e-bui* (NA)	'his wife, her husband'

Another extended meaning of *ot-* is likely 'round thing' or, at least, this meaning would seem to be involved in the following semantic chain: 'head' > 'round thing' > 'heart' > 'chest'/'back'.

(44) *ot-bo* 'back'

Abbi (2012: 376) recorded PGA *ot-bo* also with the meaning 'heart'. In PGA, but not in the Akajeru material, we also find *ot-car* 'chest, middle of the chest' (Abbi 2012: 377). Another extension of *ot-* from the meaning 'heart' is 'mind' (cf. Zamponi and Comrie 2020: 130 for an Akabea parallel).

(45) *ot-ʤete* 'shy, ashamed'

Still another extension of the prefix from the meaning 'heart' is 'soul'. The latter meaning is involved in these two semantic chains: (i) 'heart' > 'soul' > 'reflection, shadow' (see again Zamponi and Comrie 2020: 130 for a further Akabea parallel); (ii) 'heart' > 'soul' > 'dream'.

(46) *ot-ʤumulo* (NA) 'reflection, shadow' (also 'double of the sleeper' and 'photograph')

(47) *ot-ʤumu* (NA) 'dream' (n/v)

In some adjectives and verbs, *ot-* seems to be desemanticised.

(48)	*ot-lam* (NA)	'strong'
	ot-kimil (NA)	'hot; be hot' (adj/v)
	ot-ʤulu (NA)	'cold' (also noun: 'clothes')
	ot-tau (NA)	'be cold'

3.2.2 Prefix *oko-*

A prefix *oko-* is attested in the following two terms.

(49)	*oko-ʤumu*	'medicine-man' (cf. *ot-ʤumu* 'dream' (n/v))
	oko-taliŋ kolɔt (NA)	'a boy after his back was scarified in an initiation ceremony and before the turtle-eating ceremony'

The second term is the masculine counterpart of *aka-n-du kolɔt* (RB_2: 95) and this suggests that *oko-* is etymologically related to the somatic prefix *aka-* ~ *a-*, although it does not have an anatomical meaning. Perhaps *oko-* is a masculine prefix with one additional meaning shared with *aka-* ~ *a-*, specifically 'food' or 'person in a ritual restriction concerned with foods'.

3.2.3 Prefix *it-*

Another prefix with unclear meaning/function is *it-*, attested in one North Andamanese body part term also used as a kin term: *it-pet* 'belly; mother' (RB_2: 89). The root of this term likely corresponds to PGA *pɛʈ* 'swell' (v) (Abbi 2012: 379), but *it-* is not otherwise attested as a deverbal nominaliser. Radcliffe-Brown records for Akachari *pet* 'belly' (RB_2: 189), without the prefix *it-*.[9] The occurrence of *it-pet* in example (109), with an overt possessor, might suggest that *it-* derives the possessed form of the term for 'belly'. In this case, we would have a form *Ø-it-pet* meaning 'his/her belly', and not simply 'belly', as Radcliffe-Brown indicates. Also note that, in PGA, some words that seem to include the prefix *it-* have a root not found elsewhere: *it-beria* 'nice smell', *it-bi* 'yellow', *it-bitʰum* 'hook of the fishing arrow, *it-xuɖo.y* 'ring' (Abbi 2012: 360). A further recorded PGA word with *it-* is a verb: *it-kata* 'cut a big piece' (cf. *ut-kata* 'cut a very big piece') (Abbi 2013: 178).

3.2.4 Reflexive prefix *m-* ~ *n-*

A reflexive prefix *m-*, well attested in the PGA and Akachari material at our disposal, can be seen in the following North Andamanese verb. In this verb, with a meaning that implies a change of state without an agent, *m-* seems to assume the function of an anticausative marker.

(50) *e-m-pil-o* (NA) 'died' (distant past) (cf. PGA *ɛ-m-pʰil* 'die')

A pre-dental allomorph *n-* of the reflexive prefix occurs, after the somatic prefix *aka-*, in *aka-n-du kolɔt*, which is the expression used to designate a girl between the ceremony that takes place on the occasion of her first menstrual discharge and a second important initiation ceremony (see the corresponding entry in the word list in 8.1). Neither a root *du* nor a stem *aka-du* is attested in the available material of traditional Akajeru, but it should be noted that *ɖu* in PGA is a verb root meaning 'break' (cf. *ek-ɖu* 'break' (tr.) and *u-n-ɖu* 'break (of wooden items)' (tr.) (Abbi 2012: 33–4; 2013: 191) and that, as Portman (1898: 307) notes, '[w]hen an Andamanese girl menstruates she is said "To break"'.

3.2.5 *tarai- ~ tɛrai-*

The meaning of this prefix, occurring in the following two time adverbs, is also unclear.

(51) *tarai-ʧulik* 'afterwards'
tɛrai-ʧiro 'yesterday'

A phonetically similar prefix also occurs in some time adverbs of PGA and also here with an elusive meaning.

(52) PGA
tara-ʃulo 'after that'
tara-oto 'at dawn; at daybreak; early morning'

We believe that the prefix *tarai-* ~ *tɛrai-* is etymologically related to the Akabea prefix *tar-*, with a discernible basic directional meaning and also found in some nouns denoting time segments: *tar-waiɲa* 'morning; tomorrow morning', *tar-dila* 'tomorrow evening', *tar-ɔlo* 'near future' (Zamponi and Comrie 2020: 134–5).

3.2.6 Masculine suffix *-ʧiu*

A masculine suffix *-ʧiu* may be seen in just one recorded 'North Andamanese' word.

(53) *e-pota-ʧiu* (NA) 'father-in-law' (cf. *e-pota-ʧip* 'mother-in-law')

3.2.7 Feminine suffix *-ʧip*

There are four 'North Andamanese' occurrences of the feminine suffix *-ʧip* in RB_2.

(54) *arai-ʧulute-ʧip* (NA) 'younger woman of the same generation'
ot-arep-ʧip (NA) 'older woman of the same generation'
ot-otoatue-ʧip (NA) 'older woman of the same generation'
e-pota-ʧip (NA) 'mother-in-law'

Notes

1 This pigeon is very fond of the fruit of the *Ficus laccifera* (RB_2: 91).
2 Cf. also PGA *ara-mɔʈo* ~ *o-mɔʈo* 'legs' (Abbi 2012: 158).
3 It is unclear whether *ara-* derives the possessed form of the term for 'village' (and probably 'house'), similar to the somatic prefix *ot-* in PGA *ŋ-ot-ɲo* 'your house' (Abbi 2013: 161; cf. *ɲo* 'house' on p. 127).
4 Cf. Akachari <mam réb> [*sic*] 'spine' (Portman 1887: 75), for *m-om-rep* 'our spine' and PGA *ʈʰ-um-rɔnɔ* 'my ankle' recorded by Kumar (2001: 107).
5 Cf. Akachari <óm póng> 'armpit' (Portman 1887: 165) and PGA *umpʰoŋ* ~ *oŋpʰoŋ* 'armpit' (Abbi 2012: 7). Manoharan (1997: 461) has *ʈ-ɔm-ɸoŋ* 'my armpit'.
6 Cf. Akachari <óma tāū> 'foot' (Portman 1887: 33) and PGA *oma:ʈʈɔ* 'id.' (Abbi 2012: 89). There is no evidence of an allomorph *on-* or *ɔn-* of this prefix in the material of traditional Akajeru/NA at our disposal, although Abbi (2012: 4, 110, 187) and Manoharan (1997: 461) record it before the dental *t* in PGA (Abbi: *on-to* 'forearm' *on-toplo* 'alone, one'; Manoharan: *ʈ-ɔn-tow* 'my wrist'; cf. Akajeru <òng-tō> in Man (1919–23: 172)).
7 '(...) *e-tire* means young offspring of an animal or human being and therefore "a child"; *ot-tire* conveys a special reference to the child of a particular person—"his child"' (RB_2: 499).
8 Cf. also *aka-mai* 'father' with the somatic prefix *ot-* in (42) and without in (98*a*).
9 In <upetil ubeno> 'his belly in he sleep', which we interpret as follows.

(i) *Ø-u* *pet=il* *Ø-u* *beno*
3sg-PRON belly=LOC 3sg-PRON sleep
'He, on the belly, he sleeps'

4
Words

Besides morpho-syntactic words that stand alone phonologically, like all other Great Andamanese languages and many other languages of the world, Akajeru has a number of clitics that are words in the morpho-syntactic sense (given that they occupy specific syntactic positions in clauses, like other words), but not in the phonological sense. These morpho-syntactic words attach to a phonological host word proclitically (4.1.2 and 4.1.3) or enclitically (4.1.5 and 4.1.7).

4.1 Word classes

There are four well-defined major word classes in Akajeru: nouns, adjectives, verbs and adverbs. Minor categories include pronouns, a definite article, postpositions and particles.

4.1.1 Nouns

Nouns include forms that take inflectional affixes and forms that do not. Inflecting nouns are morphologically complex words that begin with a vowel-initial derivational morpheme (usually a somatic prefix). Such nouns can occur with personal prefixes that mark a pronominal possessor.

(55)	a.	*t-ot-ʧo*	'my head'
		ŋ-ot-ʧo (NA)	'your (sg.) head'
		Ø-ot-ʧo	'his/her head'
	b.	*t-ot-tire*	'my child'
		Ø-ot-tire	'his/her child'

The documentation of PGA and Akachari shows that inflecting nouns may also take the reflexive prefix, when they occur with a possessor that is coreferential with the subject of the clause.

(56) PGA

aka-mimi *Ø-ut-un-tʰire* *ta-t̪ɔpʰ-om*
SP-mother 3sg-SP-REFL-child CAUS-bathe-NPST
'The mother$_i$ is bathing her$_i$ child.'

(57) AKACHARI

Ø-ara-m-bɔitʃo *ek-ter-lul-o* *olo=ta*
3sg-SP-REFL-leg PREV-?-cut-DISTPST adze=INS
'(He$_i$) cut his$_i$ legs with an adze'

The Akajeru material does not contain similar examples.

4.1.2 Pronouns

Pronouns include personal, possessive, demonstrative and interrogative pronouns.

Personal pronouns are both free-form and proclitic. The attested free-form personal pronouns used in subject function (in affirmative clauses) are shown in Table 4.1; a dash indicates that this form is not attested. As in PGA (Abbi 2013: 169–71), free-form subject personal pronouns include a set of emphatic forms (listed in RB$_2$: 501) and a (poorly documented) set of non-emphatic forms. The forms of both sets are transparently composed of a person-number marker and a base *-io* or *-u*.

Examples containing emphatic or non-emphatic subject personal pronouns are (58), (59), (62), (76), (77) and (100–1).

(58) *ŋ-io* *t=a-tʃe-bom*
2sg-PRON.EMPH 1sgPRO=SP-accompany-NPST
'You (sg.) are accompanying me' (NA)

(59) *n-u* *beno-m*
3pl-PRO sleep-NPST
'They (are) sleeping' (NA)

Table 4.1 Free-form subject personal pronouns

	Emphatic	Non-Emphatic
1sg	*t-io*	*t-u*
2sg	*ŋ-io*	-
3sg	*Ø-io*	*Ø-u*
1pl	*m-io*	-
2pl	*ŋil-io*	-
3pl	*n-io*	*n-u*

Table 4.2 Proclitic personal pronouns

1sg	*t=*
2sg	*ŋ=*
1pl	*m=*
2pl	*ŋil=*
3pl	*n=*

The Akajeru material at our disposal does not include personal pronouns used to express other syntactic and semantic relations like Akachari *te* 'me' (direct object), *ti* 'to me' (indirect object) and *tum* 'for me' (benefactive, but also used in subject function in negated clauses, as in (83)).

Proclitic personal pronouns (also listed in RB_2: 501) are shown in Table 4.2. These have only the person-number marker. Note that these proclitic forms are segmentally identical to the prefixes in Table 4.3; the zero third person singular prefix corresponds to the absence of a third person singular proclitic form.

Proclitic personal pronouns are used exclusively before words beginning with a vowel-initial derivational prefix and, unlike free-form personal pronouns, they are attested in the function of both subject (of a nominal complement in (60), of an intransitive verb in (61) – these are the only attestations) and object (58, 62). Presumably, at least in subject function, they are even less emphatic than the non-emphatic free-form personal pronouns.

(60) *t=a-ʤeru*
1sgPRON=SP-tree_sp.
'I (am) Akajeru'

(61) *t=ot-kimil-bom*
1sgPRON=SP-hot-NPST
'I am hot' (NA)

(62) *t-io* *ŋ=arai-ʧulutu-bom*
1sg-PRON.EMPH 2sgPRO=SP-follow-NPST
'I will follow you' (NA)

In Akachari and Middle Andamanese varieties, the third person plural proclitic pronoun – *n=* in all the varieties – is attested as the marker of plural subject of a clause, assuming the function of a plural marker

(Comrie and Zamponi 2017: 43). There is a trace of this also in the North Andamanese material published by Radcliffe-Brown: *n=a-mai koloko* 'ancestors' (RB_2: 190) and *n=e-buku* 'women' (RB_2: 291).

There are only two possessive pronouns in the available Akajeru material: the first person singular *t-itʃo* and the third person singular *Ø-itʃo*, both formed by a personal prefix and a base *itʃo*. The following examples indicate that possessive pronouns are used as prehead modifiers to uninflecting nouns (63) (while inflecting nouns take a possessive prefix to mark a pronominal possessor, see 4.1.1) and also as nominal heads of their own, independently of a possessum (64).

(63) *t-itʃo* *roa*
1sg-POSS canoe
'my canoe' (NA)

(64) *kidi* *t-itʃo=bi*
DEM.PROX 1sg-POSS=COP
'This is mine' (NA)

Abbi (2013: 185) shows that in PGA possessive pronouns may occur with a suffixal variant of the reflexive prefix *m-*. This seems to happen when they mark a non-inflecting noun in a clause as being possessed by the subject of the clause.

(65) PGA
ŋil-io *ŋili-ʃɔ-m* *rɛfe=be* *raʃue-kom*
2pl-PRON.EMPH 2pl-POSS-REFL food=ABS cook-NPST
'You folks cook your own food'

The documentation of traditional Akajeru does not contain occurrences of reflexive-possessive pronouns.

Only one demonstrative pronoun was recorded: *kidi* 'this'. Its sphere is the space close to the speaker and the moment of speech (64, 66, 120).[1]

(66) *kidi* *e-nol*
DEM.PROX SP-good
'This (is) good' (NA)

And only one interrogative pronoun is found in the data: *atʃiu* 'who'. Just one example illustrating the use of this word is attested.

(67) *atʃiu* *ŋ-a-mai=bi*
who 2sg-SP-sir=COP
'Who is your (sg.) father?'

4.1.3 Definite article

The proclitic definite article *t=* codes definiteness or specificity. It occurs after the head noun but only if the following word begins with a vowel-initial derivational prefix. In the available Akajeru/North Andamanese material gathered by Radcliffe-Brown, this word is an attributive or predicative adjective (68–70, 103–4) or a possessed noun (71–3, 106–8).

(68) *ti* *t=ɛra-lobuŋ*
place DEF=SP-long
'the long place'

(69) *lau* *t=ɛr-kuro*
spirit DEF=SP-big
'the big spirit' (NA)

(70) *t-itʃo* *roa* *t=ɛr-kuro*
1sg-POSS canoe DEF=SP-big
'My canoe (is) big' (NA)

(71) *ra* *t=Ø-ot-tʃo*
pig DEF=3sg-SP-head
'the pig's head' (NA)

(72) *roa* *t=Ø-ot-tʃo*
canoe DEF=3sg-SP-head
'prow (lit. head) of the canoe'

(73) *lau* *t=Ø-ara-ɲu*
spirit DEF=3sg-SP-house
'village of the spirits' (namely 'Port Blair') (NA)

There are no occurrences of *t=* before a verb as, for example, in the Akachari sentence <Kódé wíchó kó térdu> 'Someone has broken his bow' (*kudi Ø-itʃo ko t=er-du* [DEM.PROX 3sg-POSS bow DEF=SP-break] 'That breaks his bow') recorded by Portman (1887: 183).[2]

The limited documentation of traditional Akajeru means that it is probably impossible to specify the full and precise range of the occurrence of the definite article. Abbi (2013: 156–62) analyses what is clearly a cognate of this morpheme in PGA as a prefix indicating an inanimate possessor in possessive constructions, where 'inanimate' includes dead animals, in particular with reference to severed body parts. This analysis for PGA does not, however, carry over to Akajeru/North Andamanese examples like (68–70), where the morpheme occurs before an adjective, not a possessed noun. That the use of *t=* is not constrained by the animacy of the noun it modifies in traditional North Andamanese is also suggested by the North Andamanese noun phrases in (103) and (104) and corroborated by the Akachari material in Portman (1887), where we find constructions like <ebuku tót boichal> [*sic*] 'near the woman' (*e-buku t=Ø-ot-bɔiʧɔ=l* [SP-woman DEF=SP-3sg-space_beside=LOC], lit. 'in the woman's vicinity') (p. 135).

4.1.4 Adjectives

Adjectives in Akajeru are uninflecting words denoting properties or attributes which functionally modify nouns in noun phrases (68, 69, 102–4) and can also fill the complement slot of copular clauses (66, 70, 99, 121). They seem to be numerous, as in all other Great Andamanese languages. Those which are attested cover six of the thirteen typical semantic classes of adjectives suggested in Dixon (1982: 16, 34–49; 2004: 3–5).

DIMENSION:	*e-leo* (NA) 'small', *e-lobuŋ* 'long, tall' (canoe, tree etc.), *ɛr-kuro* (NA) 'big'.
AGE:	*e-tire* (NA) 'new (of the moon)'.
VALUE:	*e-nol* 'good'.
PHYSICAL PROPERTY:	*ot-kimil* (NA) 'hot', *ot-ʤulu* (NA) 'cold', *ot-lam* (NA) 'strong'.
HUMAN PROPENSITY:	*ot-ʤete* 'shy, ashamed'.
QUANTIFICATION:	*ʧope* (NA) 'many', *deko* (NA) 'enough'.

4.1.5 Verbs

The categories expressed in the verbs of Great Andamanese languages are tense, aspect and mood (Comrie and Zamponi 2017: 65). In the available documentation of traditional Akajeru/North Andamanese we only have verbs in the indicative mood (which lacks any overt indicator) marked for non-past or one of three past tenses (see 4.3). There is also an enclitic copula verb *=bi* 'be' which, as in PGA (cf. Abbi 2013: 240), does not admit inflection.[3]

4.1.6 Adverbs

The class of adverbs in Akajeru comprises invariable words that can be both morphologically simple or composed of a derivational prefix and a root. The few attested forms are three time adverbs (*arai-ʧulu* 'after', *tarai-ʧulik* 'afterwards' and *tɛrai-ʧiro* 'yesterday') and one spatial adverb (*kulel* 'there (distant)'). The available material does not enable us to say anything about the syntax of adverbs.

4.1.7 Postpositions

Radcliffe-Brown recorded four North Andamanese postpositions: =*bi* 'ABSOLUTIVE' (which, however, he confused with the copula =*bi*; see RB_2: 502–3), =*il* 'LOCATIVE', =*ko* probably 'INESSIVE' and =*kak* 'ALLATIVE'. He also indicated that these elements 'might perhaps be regarded as suffixes as they seem never to be used except following the word to which the relation is indicated' (RB_2: 503). It is likely that they are enclitic morphemes, rather than nominal suffixes, as suggested by the following occurrences of the PGA absolutive marker =*bi* ~ =*be* after a postnominal modifier.

(74) PGA

tʰire	*mɔco*	*cɔpʰe=bi*	*er-pʰuko*
child	hen	many=ABS	SP-hit

'The child hit many hens'

(75) PGA

pʰɔr	*lobuŋ=bi*	*kʰulol*	*ɟio*
bamboo	long=ABS	there	exist

'There is a long bamboo'

The absolutive postposition =*bi* is attested only in material identified as North Andamanese. It attaches to full noun phrases and to emphatic pronouns. It is found on full noun phrase direct objects in (77) and (123). In (76) it is presumably attached to an intransitive subject, although since the verb *tuŋ* 'want' is not otherwise attested and has no known parallels in other traditional varieties of North Andamanese or in PGA, there is no independent evidence of its argument structure. It is not found with transitive subjects, whether a full noun phrase (123) or an emphatic pronoun (58, 62, 77).[4]

(76)

t-io=bi	*tuŋ-om*
1sg-PRON.EMPH =ABS	want-NPST

'I want' (NA)

(77) *Ø-io* *biu=bi* *moitʃ-om*
3sg-PRON.EMPH k.o._resin=ABS make_a_torch_of-NPST
'He is making a torch' (NA)

Here below are examples of the use of the other attested North Andamanese postpositions; they are only attested in postpositional phrases in isolation, not in clauses.

(78) *tʃup=il* (NA) 'in the basket'
(79) *ŋ-oŋ-kɔro=ko* (NA) 'in your (sg.) hand'
(80) *lautitʃe=kak* (NA) 'to Port Blair'

4.1.8 Particles

The North Andamanese negative suffix *-pu* mentioned by Radcliffe-Brown (RB_2: 503) is, in fact, a negator particle which has (or can have) scope over copular clauses, as illustrated by the following examples from PGA and Akachari, where it precedes the copula verb 'be'. Unfortunately, there are no relevant Akajeru examples.

(81) AKACHARI
kidi *tʃokbi* *pu=bi*
DEM.PROX turtle sp. NEG=COP
'This is not a turtle'

(82) PGA
ʈ^h-ut-bɔ *nɔl* *p^{h}o=be*
1sg-SP-heart nice NEG=COP
'I do not like' (lit. 'My heart is not nice')

It should be noted that negation of verbal clauses in PGA and Akachari is by means of the same negator, but the verbal clause appears in the subject slot of a negated existential copular clause. The verb of the verbal clause occurs in a non-finite form which excludes TAM markers.

(83) AKACHARI
t-um *ŋ=ir-tiliu* *pu=bi*
1sg-PRON 2PRON=SP-see NEG=COP
'I cannot see you'

(84) PGA
ɟicer=bi *cer-om* *ʈ^h=ut-cone* *p^{h}o=be*
rain=ABS rain-NPST 1sgPRON=SP-go NEG=COP
'I will not leave since it is raining'

A further North Andamanese particle recorded by Radcliffe-Brown is perhaps the human noun collective marker *koloko*. Manoharan (1989: 61) describes it as 'bound morpheme to the common human nouns'. Abbi (2012: 44) represents it as an independent phonological word: *at*^{h}*ire kɔːrlɔxo* 'children'. Radcliffe-Brown (RB_2) writes it now as if it were a suffix (<n'a-mai-koloko> 'ancestors'; p. 190), now as an independent word (<Kelera buliu koloko> 'a local group of the Akabo'; p. 28).

4.2 Compound words

All the compounds in the data are nominal and have two components, at least one of which is a noun. The compounds that follow consist of two nouns that provide different descriptions for the same referent.

(85) *kɔrotʃop* 'structure erected across a dancing ground'[5] (NA)
kɔro 'shredded palm-leaf fibre'
tʃop 'tree sp.'

(86) *terkobito balo* 'creeper sp.: *Pothos sandens*' (NA)
terkobito 'centipede'
balo 'creeper'

The following compound is also a combination of two nouns. The second noun is a hyperonym of the first one here.

(87) *tɔlodu* 'white clay'
tɔl 'white clay' (a synonym of *tɔlodu*)
odu 'k.o. clay'

A further type of nominal compound found in the material corresponds to a possessive construction of type B in Chapter 5 with a possessor that precedes a possessed noun. The components of this type of compound in some cases (90–2) are written as separate words by Radcliffe-Brown.

(88) *tʃokbidʒo* 'turtle-eating ceremony' (NA)
tʃokbi 'turtle'
dʒo 'food'

(89) *kimildʒo* 'turtle-eating ceremony' (NA)
kimil 'a boy or girl during the turtle-eating ceremony'
dʒo 'food'

(90) *timiku lau* (NA) 'spirit that haunts the jungles'
timiku 'forest, jungle' (cf. (94))
lau 'spirit'

(91) *bido tetʃ lau* (NA) 'spirit of the *Calamus* leaf'
bido 'palm sp.: *Calamus tigrinus*'
tetʃ 'leaf'
lau 'spirit'

(92) *ino kɔlo* 'mollusc sp.'
ino 'water'
kɔlo 'mollusc sp.'

Example (93) shows a compound including a noun and a verb. The noun bears an object relation to the verb.

(93) *biumɔitʃ* 'torch of resin' (NA)
biu 'k.o. resin'
mɔitʃ 'make a torch of'

Another three or, perhaps, four nouns found in the data are non-canonical compounds. One (94) or, perhaps, two (94, 95) are formations including an independent noun and a bound nominal root which, in other contexts, occurs with a somatic prefix attached.

(94) *timiku* (NA) 'forest, jungle'[6]
ti 'place'
miku – cf. *ir-miku* 'face, forehead'

(95) *piletʃar* 'high-tide'
pile – cf. PGA *e-pʰile* 'high-tide'
tʃar – cf. *tʃari* 'salt water'

Another compound (96), designating a species of snake, includes a root *ɔr* and the generic term for 'snake'.

(96) *ɔrtʃubi* 'snake sp.: *Ophiophagus elaps*'[7]
ɔr
tʃubi 'snake'

The remaining noun is possibly a cranberry compound including an obscure element that does not seem to belong to the nominal lexicon of any North Andamanese variety.

(97) *tɔrodiu* (NA) 'full sun, middle part of the day'
tɔro '?'
diu 'sun'

4.3 Inflection

As indicated above in 4.1.1, inflecting nouns mark person and number of the possessor by prefixes.

(98) a. *t-a-mai* 'my father'
ŋ-a-mai 'your (sg.) father'
Ø-aka-mai 'his/her father'
n-a-mai 'their father'
b. *t-a-mimi* 'my mother'
Ø-aka-mimi (NA) 'his/her mother'

The possessive prefixes (based on RB_2: 501) are shown in Table 4.3; they are identical to the person-number markers occurring in personal pronouns (4.1.2).

The attested verbal forms of Akajeru, as indicated above (4.1.5), show a primary temporal distinction between non-past and past. For the latter, a further three-way distinction is found.

The marker of non-past tense is the suffix *-bom* ~ *-kom* ~ *-om* ~ *-m*. It locates a situation indifferently at or after the present moment. Allomorphs are idiosyncratic and unpredictable (see Table 4.4).

One of the three past tenses is unmarked. Presumably, as in PGA (Abbi 2013: 233), this is a generic past irrespective of the length of time between the past situation and the time of the utterance.

(99) *deko* *b=ɛra-lio*
enough COP=SP-finish
'(It is) enough. (It) is finished' (NA)

Table 4.3 Possessive prefixes

	SG	PL
1	*t-*	*m-*
2	*ŋ-*	*ŋil-*
3	*Ø-*	*n-*

Table 4.4 Non-past form of some Akajeru/NA verbs

Verb	Akajeru/NA
'accompany'	*aka-ʧe-***bom** (NA)
'be cold'	*ot-tau-***bom** (NA)
'do, make, work'	*ʧato-***bom** (NA)
'follow'	*arai-ʧulutu-***bom**
'be hot'	*ot-kimil-***bom** (NA)
'talk'	*ar-***bom** (NA)
'have in adoption'	*oiʧolo-***kom** (NA)
'marry, be married'	*e-bui-***om** (NA)
'want'	*tuŋ-***om** (NA)
'sing'	*e-ur-***om** (NA)
'make a torch'	*moiʧ-***om** (NA)
'sleep'	*beno-***m** (NA)

Another past tense is marked by means of the suffix *-ba*. We again presume that this suffix has the same value of immediate past marker as PGA *-a* ~ *-e* ~ *-be* ~ *-ka* ~ *-ke*, used to refer to a situation that took place a few hours prior to the time of the utterance (Abbi 2012: 233).

(100) *Ø-u* *beno-ba*
3SG-PRO sleep-IMMPST
'He slept' (NA)

(101) *t-u* *boto-ba*
1SG-PRO fall-IMMPST
'I fell' (NA)

The third attested past tense is marked by the suffix *-o* (50). The suffix appears as the equivalent of the PGA marker of distant past *-o* used for any other event beyond the time period covered by the immediate past (Abbi 2012: 233)

There is no evidence in the sparse material of traditional Akajeru/ North Andamanese of the past used for narration that Abbi (2012: 233) observed in PGA.

Notes

1 Note that in PGA demonstrative pronouns indicate three degrees of distance: (i) near the speaker (*k*^{h}*idi*), (ii) near the hearer (*k*^{h}*udi*) and (iii) away from the speaker and the hearer (*ɖi* ‘VISIBLE’ (sg.) and *ɖu* ~ *ɖuio* ~ *u* ‘INVISIBLE’ (sg.)) (Abbi 2013: 211).

2 The Akachari documentation also contains some occurrences of *t*= attached to the third person singular possessive pronoun *iʧo* within possessive noun phrases of the type that, in Chapter 5, we call A; e.g.: <Chío télem taichāū tíbé> ‘Where is the best place for shells?’ (*ʧio telem t=Ø-iʧɔ ti=bi* [where shell DEF=3sg-POSS place=COP] ‘Where is the place of the shells’) (Portman 1887: 127) and <Tí jéóbí tíchó tí pubí> ‘There is no place to cook’ (*taʤeo=bi t=Ø-iʧo ti pu=bi* [fish=ABS DEF=3sg-POSS place NEG=COP] ‘There is not the place of fish’) (Portman 1887: 177) (to compare with <Án íchó étíré, étárí, ébuku?> ‘Is this child a boy, or a girl?’ (*an Ø-iʧo e-tire e-taru e-buku* [Y/N 3sg-POSS SP-child SP-male SP-female] ‘Is his child a boy or a girl?’) (Portman 1887: 193)). The Akajeru corpus does not include analogous examples.

3 =*bi* is always an independent word orthographically in Radcliffe-Brown’s fragments of Akajeru/NA, but Portman (1887: 95–191, *passim*) transcribes its Akachari equivalent -*bi* ~ -*be* attached to the preceding morphological word.

4 In PGA =*bi* is attached to intransitive subjects and (direct) objects (Abbi 2013: 116).

5 See the item *kɔroʧop* in the Akajeru–English word list (section 8.1) for a description of the denotatum of this word.

6 Cf. *tɔŋmugu* ‘coast’ in Akabea, composed of the bound roots *tɔŋ* (see *on-tɔŋ* ‘leaf’) and *mugu* (see *ig-mugu* ‘face, forehead’) (Zamponi and Comrie 2020: 237).

7 Radcliffe-Brown writes this as a single word, <o̱r-čubi> (RB$_2$: 124) or <or-čubi> (RB$_2$: 317, 373, 484), while Portman (1887: 73) records the Akachari equivalent as two words <ór chubí>, similarly to the corresponding terms in Akabea and Opuchikwar (<wára jóbo> and <wára chupe>). Abbi (2012: 242) writes the PGA equivalent as a single word, and our interpretation of the accompanying audio recording is as a single word with initial stress. We follow the one-word analysis in the main text.

5
Noun phrases

In the noun phrase of Akajeru (as of all other Great Andamanese dialects and languages; see Comrie and Zamponi 2017: 69), possessive pronouns and nominal possessors precede the head noun (63, 70–3, 105–17), while the definite article and adjectives follow it (68–73, 102–4, 106–8, 121, 122).[1]

(102) *reɲa* *ʧope*
possession many
'many possessions' (NA)

The definite article occurs immediately after the head noun and thus separates the head noun from a following adjective (68, 69, 103, 104).

(103) *kɔroin* *t=ɛr-kuro*
dugong DEF=SP-big
'the big dugong' (NA)

(104) *ra* *t=ɛr-kuro*
pig DEF=SP-big
'the big pig' (NA)

Regarding noun phrases with a full nominal possessor, Akajeru features two different constructions depending on the inflectional possibilities of the possessed constituent. In both possessive constructions, the possessed constituent follows the possessor noun phrase.

Type A. One type of possessive construction is that in which the possessed element corresponds to an uninflecting noun and, between the possessor and the possessed, there is a third person singular possessive pronoun, presumably even when the possessed item is plural in number (as in the other Great Andamanese languages; Comrie and Zamponi

2017: 70).[2] This type of construction codes alienable possession. Possessed nouns found in it denote referents of various kinds and include all the uninflecting forms of the nominal lexicon except body part and plant part terms. The possessive construction in question expresses a relation where the possessed item is not an integral part of the possessing entity.

(105) *bora* *Ø-itʃo* *roa*
Bora 3sg-POSS canoe
'Bora's (♂) canoe' (NA)

Type B. The second type of possessive construction is that in which the possessed corresponds to an inflecting noun or an uninflecting noun denoting a body part or a plant part. In this type, the possessed noun, indexed by the zero realisation of the third person singular possessive prefix if inflecting, directly follows the possessor noun phrase without further, explicit markers of the possession relation.

(106) *lau* *t=Ø-ɛr-tʃo*
spirit DEF=3sg-SP-head
'skull of the dead person' (NA)

(107) *ra* *t=Ø-ot-betʃ*
pig DEF=3sg-SP-hair
'pig's hair' (NA)

(108) *ɔrtʃubi* *t=Ø-ɛra-bat*
snake sp. DEF=3sg-SP-tail
'design of zig-zag lines painted on the body with white clay (lit. snake's tail)'

(109) *rea* *Ø-it-pet*
Rea 3sg-?-swell
'Rea's (♂) mother' (NA) (also 'Rea's belly')

(110) *bora* *Ø-ot-tire*
Bora 3sg-SP-child
'Bora's (♂) child' (NA)

(111) *tarai* *Ø-ɛra-poŋ*
Tarai 3sg-SP-hole
'Tarai's (♂) cave'

When the possessed item is an uninflecting noun this construction may be said to code inalienable possession. Specifically, it appears to express a relation where the possessed item and possessing entity are regarded as integrally and essentially part of each other.[3]

(112) *tʃokbi* *tʃiro*
turtle sp. liver
'turtle's liver'

(113) *tʃokbi* *tei*
turtle sp. blood
'turtle's blood' (NA)

(114) *lau* *tɔi*
spirit bone
'bones of a dead person' (NA)

(115) *remu* *tɔi*
iron bone
'piece of iron' (lit. 'bone of the iron') (NA)

(116) *ɛr-tap* *betʃ*
lower_jaw hair
'beard'

(117) *pɔitʃo* *tomo*
tree_sp. wood
'wood of the *Sterculia* tree' (NA)

There are also some examples of appositional constructions in the data, namely apposition of a title or kin term with a personal name (118) and apposition of two nouns, the second of which is needed for the appropriate identification of the denotatum of the first noun (119).[4]

(118) *maya lirtʃitmo* 'Sir Kingfisher'
mimi biliku 'Madam Biliku'
e-tire bora (NA) 'the child Bora (♂)'

(119) *biliku bɔto* 'north-east wind' (*biliku* is also the name of a female supernatural being)
tarai bɔto 'south-west wind' (*tarai* is also the name of a male supernatural being)

Notes

1 The corpus of traditional Akajeru does not contain examples of noun phrases with a demonstrative modifying a following head noun like Akachari *kudi ebuku* 'that woman' (Portman 1887: 161).
2 Cf. PGA *ɖun Ø-iʃo ko* (DEM.DIST.INV.PL 3sg-POSS bow) 'their bow' (Abbi 2013: 130).
3 The definite article cannot modify an uninflecting possessor since the latter lacks a vowel-initial derivational prefix. (No vowel-initial inalienably possessed noun is known.) Although this restriction on the use of the definite article does not occur in Akabea (see *baraidʒ la lagia* [village DEF near] 'the nearby village'; Portman (1887: 100)), the definite article is also not used in this language in possessive constructions with a possessor that combines with an inalienably possessed uninflecting noun: *tʃauga ta* 'bone of the dead person', but *tʃauga l=Ø-ot-tʃeta* [dead_person DEF=3-SP-head] 'head of the dead person' (Portman 1887: 210).
4 Cf. also Akabo *uluku tʃubi* 'snake sp.' (RB_2: 97) (PGA *ulukʰu* 'king cobra'; Abbi 2012: 395).

6 Clauses

Clauses may be copular or verbal. The attested copular clauses, with and without the enclitic copula *=bi*, express relations of identity, attribution and existence. The complement is a noun phrase in identity relation in (60, 64, 120) and an adjective in attribution relation in (66, 70, 99, 121), while (122) illustrates existence.

(120) *kidi* *kɔroin=bi*
DEM.PROX dugong=COP
'This is a dugong' (NA)

(121) *Ø-e-tomo* *t=ot-lam*
3sg-SP-flesh DEF-SP-strong
'His/her flesh (is) strong' (NA)

(122) *ino* *ot-kimil=bi*
water SP-hot=COP
'There is hot water' (NA)

The basic constituent order of intransitive verbal clauses is subject-verb (59, 61, 100, 101). In transitive verbal clauses, the subject constituent precedes the object constituent and the object constituent precedes the verb (58, 62, 77, 123) (see also RB_2: 504).

(123) *buyo* *ʤo=bi* *e-ur-om*
Buio song=ABS SP-sing-NPST
'Buio (♂) is singing a song' (NA)

The only interrogative clause recorded for Akajeru is the copular content question in (67) with the interrogative pronoun *aʧiu* 'who' in initial position. We have no examples of negative or imperative clauses. Complex sentences are also unattested.

7
Present-day Great Andamanese, Akajeru and the other traditional dialects of North Andaman

A major consequence of the decrease of population that affected the Great Andamanese groups after the establishment of the British penal settlement at Port Blair in 1858 was that what were formerly distinct and often hostile communities gradually ended up merging together. 'The different languages have become corrupt, and some tribes have adopted customs of other tribes and have abandoned their own', writes Radcliffe-Brown (RB_2: 19) in reference to the beginning of the twentieth century. Manoharan (1989: 138) indicates that in this process of merging, minor groups started adopting the speech and other cultural traits of the majority group, and recalls that, through its history since the 1901 census record, the Akajeru were the numerically dominant group.[1] Hence it is not surprising that PGA is primarily a direct descendant of the pre-contact dialect of the Akajeru. In this regard, Basu observes what follows in the 1950s.

> The position of the Great Andamanese being such, when some of their clans have become extinct, and some are dwindling, and when the small number of their people have to reside together, irrespective of their differences in sept and dialect, and when they have very little independent entity in political and economic lives, they have naturally taken up one dialect as 'Standard' among themselves. It is the majority-speaking Jeru dialect, which has been recognised as the 'Standard dialect' by them although they are very much conscious of the individuality of their own dialects. (Basu 1952: 57)

It has, however, been pointed out by different authors that PGA cannot be considered simply the contemporary form of the speech of the Akajeru, but rather an Akajeru-based variety containing elements of all the other traditional dialects of North Andamanese.

> The present Andamanese language it is quite obvious, is the retention of a language of the Northern tribes. A comparison of the present Andamanese language to that of Portman's 1898 work[2] support [*sic*] this view. But the general conclusion arrived at is that 'the present Andamanese language is a mixed language, i.e. a creole predominantly dominated by the older Jeru language'. (Manoharan 1989: 140)

> The Great Andamanese as it is at present represents only the North-Andaman dialect of Jeru with possible mixture of Cari (or Sare as they call it now), Kora (or Khora) and little of Pucikwar (or Pujjukar). It cannot be proved at this time as to how much of mixed elements have emerged in Jeru from other dialects until a comparative study is undertaken which is possible only if one relies on the syntactic data provided by Portman in his *Manual*. (Choudhary 2006: 15)

> Very soon they all [the Great Andamanese] spoke one language, Jero with some words from the languages of the other tribes completely assimilated into it. (Narang 2008: 316)

> PGA draws its lexicon from Jeru, Sare, Khora and Bo, but is primarily based on the grammar of Jeru. As the present form is the amalgam of four languages, the author has deliberately avoided naming this form of the language 'Jeru' as this will unnecessarily place an arbitrary emphasis on one language over the others. (Abbi 2013: 10)

In this short chapter, we will attempt to evaluate the validity of these affirmations by comparing the scarce available data of traditional Akajeru with those available for PGA drawn, mainly, from Abbi's recent grammar (2013) and dictionary (2012) of this variety.

Phonetically, the occurrence of a fricative [ʃ] or [s] in the speech of most of the last speakers or rememberers of PGA is the most significant innovation we may observe. No word of a traditional dialect of North Andamanese was recorded with one of these sounds. The fricatives [ʃ] and [s] occur only word-initially and word-medially and correspond, in the traditional dialects of North Andamanese, to the sound transcribed by Radcliffe-Brown with <č> and which, as indicated in 2.1.1, may be the palatal affricate [ʧ] or the palatal stop [c].[3]

Meaning	PGA	Akajeru	Akachari	Akabo
'k.o. basket'	*ʃup ~ sup ~ suːp*	<čup>	<chup>	-
'snake'	*ʃubi ~ subi*	<čubi>	<chubí>	<čubi>
'who'	*aʃiu*	<ačiu>	<áchu>	-

Abbi (2013: 47) indicates that the palato-alveolar fricative [ʃ] occurs in the speech of individuals of Akajeru background, while the alveolar fricative [s] occurs only in the speech of a woman of mixed Akachari and Akakhora background. According to Manoharan (1989: 32, 172), people descended from the former Akachari group have retained the palatal stop [c], while people of Akajeru background use [s]. Manoharan suggests that the failure to distinguish [s] in the transcription of Akajeru 'is nothing but a mistake' on Radcliffe-Brown's part. We find this hard to believe, however, since [s] is perceptually quite distinct from [ʧ] or [c] for a native speaker of English and Radcliffe-Brown, in writing Akajeru, made use of a phonetic transcription, albeit simplified, based on the 'Anthropos' alphabet of Wilhelm Schmidt (Schmidt 1907). It is very likely that the idiosyncratic replacement of [ʧ] ~ [c] with [ʃ] or [s] is a post-contact phenomenon, perhaps due to influence of Hindi, as Basu (1952: 61) indicates.[4]

It is not unusual for the same word to differ in vowel correspondences in the North Andamanese dialects (specifically in the better attested Akajeru and Akachari). In the following cases, the PGA equivalent of such words with different vowel qualities in Akajeru (or Radcliffe-Brown's 'North Andamanese') and Akachari has the same vowel as the Akajeru (or 'North Andamanese') form.[5]

Meaning	PGA	Akajeru/NA	Akachari
'k.o. clay'	*oḍu*	*odu*	*oto*
'rain' (n)	*ɟicɛr*	*ʤiʧɛr* (NA)	*ʤoʧer*
'small'	*eleo*	*eleo* (NA)	*lau*

But there are also cases in which a PGA word exhibits the same vocalism as its Akachari equivalent rather than its Akajeru counterpart.

Meaning	PGA	Akajeru/NA	Akachari
'finish'	*araliu*	*ɛralio* (NA)	*araliu*
'frog sp.'	*p^horube*	*pɔrubi* (NA)	*porube*
'there (distant)'	*k^hulol*	*kulel*	*kulol*
'tree sp.: *Sterculia macrophylla*'	*p^hoco*	*pɔiʧo*	*poʧo*

In yet other cases, more numerous than the previous ones, a PGA form differs from both its Akajeru and Akachari equivalent in the quality of one of its vowels.

MEANING	PGA	AKAJERU/NA	AKACHARI
'canoe'	*ro:ɔ*	*roa*	*roa*
'child'	*uttʰire*	*ottire* (NA)	*ottire*
'fly sp.'	*pʰulɛmu*	*pulimi* (NA)	*pulimu*
'long, tall'	*iloboŋ*	*elobuŋ*	*elobuŋ*
'mother-of-pearl shell'	*bo*	*be*	*be*
'salt water'	*sare*	*ʧari* (NA)	*ʧari*
'shy, ashamed'	*uɟɟete*	*otʤete*	*otʤete*
'sky'	*ʈao ~ ʈɔo ~ ʈɔ:*	*tau*	*tau*
'sling'	*ceba*	*ʧiba*	*ʧiba*
'spine'	*onrɛ:p*	*omrap*	*omrep*
'spirit'	*lao*	*lau*	*lau*
'a supernatural being' (♂)	*tʰarae*	*tarai*	*tarai*
'tree sp.'[6]	*cɔlekʰi*	*ʧoleke*	*ʧoleke*

Few recurring vowel correspondences may, however, be extracted from the latter forms:

Akajeru, Akachari *a* : PGA ɔ (see 'canoe' and 'sky')
Akajeru, Akachari *au* : PGA *ao* (see 'sky' and 'spirit')
Akajeru, Akachari *i* : PGA *e* (see 'salt water', 'sling' and 'a supernatural being')[7]

In the case of the name of the supernatural being, the final vowel is also *i* in the forms of this name used by the Akabo and Akakhora (RB_2: 147, 199). We may therefore regard the lowering of *i* to *e* seen in PGA *tʰarae* as a possible further development that took place in post-contact times.

Rarely, pronunciation differences between PGA and the traditional forms of Akajeru and Akachari concern the consonant sounds in words. In this regard, the only examples we have noted are that the name of the imperial pigeon is *merit* in PGA but *mirid* both in Akajeru and Akachari and that the name of a species of tree (*Dipterocarpus laevis*) is *kɔrɔiɲ* in PGA and, apparently, *kɔrɔin* again both in Akajeru and Akachari.

In the few cases in which an Akajeru word differs completely from its Akachari equivalent, we may note that the PGA corresponding form is identical or very similar to the Akajeru word.

MEANING	PGA	AKAJERU	AKACHARI
'bad'	*ecae*	*etʃai*	*ebekedeŋ*
'fingernail'	*oŋkara*	*oŋkara*	*kudemu*
'wife, husband'	*eboe*	*ebui*	*ebuku* 'wife', *etaru* 'husband'

There could be one exception, however. The term for 'moon' is *ɖulɔ* both in PGA and, probably, Akachari (cf. <dolāū> in Portman (1887: 51)), but it was recorded as *tʃirikli* in Akajeru. The latter form was also gathered by Portman for Akachari (cf. <chírīklí> 'moon' in Portman (1887: 191)), but it is unclear whether it is a perfect synonym of *ɖulɔ* and also whether the Akajeru used it.

Morphologically, the only documented difference between traditional Akajeru and PGA seems to concern the use of the somatic prefix *ot-* with terms that denote human beings when they are possessed (3.2.1.6). The last speakers or rememberers of PGA do not seem to add a somatic prefix to terms referring to human beings that already contain a somatic prefix: *ʈʰ-ara-sulutʰu* 'my younger brother/sister' (Abbi 2013: 145, 154) (cf. Akajeru *Ø-ot-arai-tʃulute* 'his/her younger brother').[8] In the possessed form of the term for 'child', however, they use the somatic prefix *ot-* ~ *ɔt-* ~ *ut-* instead of the somatic prefix *a-* (*e-* in Akajeru), exactly like the speakers of traditional Akajeru/NA: *a-tʰire* 'child', *ʈ-ut-tʰire* 'my child' (Abbi 2012: 44) (cf. example (41) in section 3.2.1.6).[9]

No difference between PGA and Akajeru emerges in the area of syntax based on our (scanty) knowledge of the latter. Note, however, the very different analyses of the element *t=* or *t-* (proclitic definite article in our analysis of Akajeru, section 4.1.3; prefix indicating an inanimate possessor in Abbi's analysis of PGA (Abbi 2013: 156–62)).

To sum up, we believe that the claim that Akajeru represents the base of PGA is adequately supported by the linguistic data. In the idiolects of the last speakers or rememberers of PGA there are, probably, also a number of Akachari words as well as words that do not appear either in Akajeru nor in Akachari and might belong to Akabo or Akakhora, the two other traditional dialects of North Andamanese of which we know almost nothing. Interestingly, PGA shows two probable post-contact developments in certain lexical forms, namely the deaffrication/depalatalisation of [tʃ] ~ [c] to [ʃ] or [s] and the lowering of [i] to [e].

Notes

1 Between 1976 and 1982, there were four families who claimed Akajeru descent, two families who claimed Akabo descent and three old men living without wife who claimed Akachari, Opuchikwar or Akarbale descent (Manoharan and Gnanasundaram 2007: 27).

2 Portman (1898).

3 Cf. also the Akakhora toponym <Čaroŋa>.

4 'Man, Portman, and Brown [*sic*] noticed that the Andamanese possessed no sibilant sounds. But intently looking for it, the writer noticed sounds in their languages exactly similar to the palatal sibilants. (...) These sibilants are clearly the development of the affricate sounds mainly as a result of their constant touch with these sounds in Hindi (Hindustani)'.

5 In some cases, <ai> stands for a single mid front vowel in Portman's transcription of Akachari: cf. <tainjíwu> 'dance' (Portman 1887: 25) (*t=e-n-ʤiu* 'I dance', but note <eng jíwu> (*e-n-ʤiu*) 'earthquake' on p. 29) and <érain chék> 'make noise' (Portman 1887: 53) (*er-en-ʧek* 'id', with the same prefixal sequence of <éren teko> (*er-en-teko*) 'hum'; Portman 1887: 39). It is therefore probable that the Akachari terms for 'hair' and 'leaf' had a /e/ or /ɛ/ just like their PGA and Akajeru or 'North Andamanese' equivalents, not a diphthong /ai/: Akachari <ót baich> 'hair' (Portman 1887: 167), PGA *otbec* ~ *otbɛc*, Akajeru *otbeʧ* 'hair'; <taich> 'leaf' (Portman 1887: 35, 69 139, 159), PGA *tec* ~ *tɛc*, 'North Andamanese' *teʧ*. Cf. also Akachari <étaichí> 'give' (Portman 1887: 155) and PGA *e-tɛʃe*.

6 *Pterocarpus dalbergioides*. This name is recorded as *chawleke* by Awasthi (1991: 277).

7 Cf. also the following forms whose Akachari equivalent is not attested: Akajeru *oŋtɔi* 'wrist' : PGA *oŋʈɔe* 'id.'; 'North Andamanese' and Akabo *ɲuri* 'fish sp.: *Plotosus* sp.' : PGA *ɲure* 'id.'; 'North Andamanese' *kiʤeri* 'wander' : PGA *kiɟire* 'id.'.

8 We emphasise that the use in Akajeru of the prefix *ot-* with terms that denote human beings is far from clear. As indicated in 3.2.1.6, it appears connected with possession, but the details remain elusive. We do not, for example, know the precise semantics of *Ø-ot-e-bui* 'his wife, her husband', which Radcliffe-Brown indicates as a variant form of *Ø-e-bui* (example (43)), as well as that of *ŋ-ot-a-mai* in (42), which we may compare with *ŋ-a-mai* 'your (sg.) father' in (98*a*).

9 The bare stem *tʰire* is also used as the non-possessed form of 'child' in PGA (Abbi 2012: 44, Abbi 2013: 68). Also note that Manoharan (1989: 116) records the two non-possessed forms of this noun as *ɛthi:rɛ* and *thi:rɛ*.

8
Word list

This chapter provides a list of all the words of the traditional speech of the Akajeru that were recorded (section 8.1), excluding personal names and toponyms (several of which are listed in section 1.1), together with an English–Akajeru finder list (section 8.2). The word list also includes all the items recorded by Radcliffe-Brown (RB_2) as 'North Andamanese' words (and presumably also used by the Akajeru, at least in the vast majority of cases). It presents our morphemic analysis of multimorphemic forms and the meaning of each Akajeru or 'North Andamanese' word, as well as all attestations in the original source(s) from which they were drawn, in the form in which they appear there. In this way, the word list allows the reader to trace back our analyses to the original source material.

Entries in the word list are organised as follows. We first list the shape of the headword, in the semi-phonemic transcription described in section 2.4. This is followed, in the order indicated, by:

- **(i)** the headword's morphemic analysis (only when the headword is multimorphemic);
- **(ii)** an abbreviation, in parentheses, that indicates whether the headword was recorded as an Akajeru or 'North Andamanese' form (or both);
- **(iii)** an indication of the part of speech (grammatical category);
- **(iv)** the headword's meaning or meanings as they can be derived from the source(s) that attest it; in the case of a grammatical morpheme, the morpheme label is given in small capitals.

This basic information is followed in turn by:

- **(v)** a list of all attestations of the headword in the source(s) in which it occurs and, sometimes, by one or both of **(vi)** and **(vii)**;
- **(vi)** the known cognate form in PGA and/or Akachari;

(vii) a note that may indicate one or more related forms recorded in the word list or supply comments of an ethnographic or other nature.

Subentries, for phrasal expressions, are indented under the main entry, with the same organisation as main entries.

Headwords are entered following this sequencing of symbols: *a, b, d, ʤ, e, ɛ, k, l, m, n, ŋ, ɲ, o, ɔ, p, r, t, ʧ, y*.

8.1 Akajeru word list

air (AKJ) *n*

Foam on a rough sea

Attestations:

(1) <air> 'foam on a rough sea' (RB_2: 193)

akaʤeru |aka-ʤeru| (AKJ) *n*

Akajeru

Attestations:

(1) <t'a-ǰeru> 'I am Aka-Jeru' (*t=a-ʤeru* 'id.') (RB_2: 24)

Notes:

Cf. **ʤeru**.

akakimil |aka-kimil| (NA) *n*

Condition of a boy or girl who is passing through the initiation ceremonies

Attestations:

(1) <aka-kimil> 'condition [of a youth or girl from the time of commencement of the initiation ceremonies]' (RB_2: 101), 'a person (...) who has just been through one of the initiation ceremonies' (RB_2: 123), 'a youth or girl who is passing through the initiation ceremonies' (RB_2: 267)

Notes:

Cf. **ɛrkimil, kimil, kimil ʤo, otkimil**$_1$ and **otkimil**$_2$.

akakimil kolɔt |aka-kimil kolɔt| (NA) *n*

A boy or girl who is passing through the initiation ceremonies

Attestations:

(1) <aka-kimil kolo̱t> 'a person who is in this condition' (RB_2: 101)

Notes:
The meaning of **kolɔt** is uncertain, perhaps 'boy, girl'.

akamai |aka-mai| (AKJ, NA) *n*
Father

Attestations:
(1) <aka-mai> 'his father' (*Ø-aka-mai* 'id.') (RB_2: 54), 'father' (RB_2: 190), <t'a-mai> 'my father' (*t-a-mai* 'id.') (RB_2: 54, 66), <ŋ'a-mai> 'your father' (*ŋ-a-mai* 'id.') (RB_2: 54), <n'a-mai> 'their father, their fathers' (*n-a-mai* 'id.') (RB_2: 54) (AKJ)
(2) <aka-mai> 'his father' (RB_2: 54), <Bora aka-mai> 'Bora's father' (*bora Ø-aka-mai* 'id.') (RB_2: 54), <Rea aka-mai> 'Rea's father' (*rea Ø-aka-mai*) (RB_2: 89) (NA)

Comparisons:
PGA *t̪ʰamai* 'my father' (Abbi 2013: 150); Akachari <á mái> [*sic*] 'father' (Portman 1887: 31)

Notes:
Cf. **mai**
akamai koloko |aka-mai koloko| (NA)
Ancestors

Attestations:
(1) <n'a-mai-koloko> 'ancestors' (*n=a-mai koloko* 'id.') (RB_2: 190)
akamai otaraiʧulute |aka-mai Ø-ot-arai-ʧulute| (lit. 'younger person of the same generation of the father') (NA)
Younger paternal uncle

Attestations:
(1) <ŋ'ot-a-mai ot-arai-čulute> 'thy father's younger brother' (*ŋ-ot-a-mai Ø-ot-arai-ʧulute*) (RB_2: 56)

Notes:
otamai otaraiʧulute seems to be the possessed form of this kin expression (see section 3.2.1.6).

akamimi |aka-mimi| (AKJ, NA) *n*
Mother

Attestations:
(1) <t'-a-mimi> 'my mother' (*t-a-mimi* 'id.') (RB_2: 66) (AKJ)
(2) <aka-mimi> 'his mother' (RB_2: 54) (NA)

Comparisons:

PGA *ṯ*^{h}*amimi* 'my mother' (Abbi 2013: 150); Akachari <ta mémí> 'id.' (*t-a-mimi* 'my mother') (RB_2: 51)

akamimi akamai |aka-mimi Ø-aka-mai| (lit. 'mother's father') (AKJ, NA)

Maternal grandfather

Attestations:

(1) <aka-mimi aka-mai> 'his mother's father' (*aka-mimi Ø-aka-mai*) (AKJ) (RB_2: 69)

(2) <t'a-mimi aka-mai> 'my mother's father' (*t-a-mimi Ø-aka-mai* 'id.') (NA) (RB_2: 69)

Notes:

Cf. **mimi**.

akandu kolɔt |aka-n-du kolɔt| (NA) *n*

A girl between the ceremony that takes place on the occasion of her first menstrual discharge and the turtle-eating ceremony

Attestations:

(1) <aka-ndu-kolo̲t> 'girl [after this ceremony]' (RB_2: 94, 95, 101)

Notes:

du is likely the verb root 'break' (cf. 3.2.4). The meaning of **kolɔt** is uncertain, perhaps 'boy, girl'.

akanɔro |aka-nɔro| (AKJ) *n*

Throat

Attestations:

(1) <âkà-nōro> 'throat' (M: 172)

akaodu |aka-odu| (NA) *n*

Mourner

Attestations:

(1) <aka-odu> 'mourner' (RB_2: 111, 289), 'a person who is in mourning' (RB_2: 122)

Comparisons:

Akachari <ér otó> 'in mourning' (Portman 1887: 109)

Notes:

'The essentials of mourning are (1) the use of clay (*odu*), and (2) abstention from certain foods, from dancing, and from the use of white clay (*to̲l*) and red paint. (…) every adult in the camp covers himself or herself with clay on the death of an adult member of the community, but when this wears off, or is washed off in the course of two or three days, it is not renewed. The near relatives retain this covering of clay for many weeks, constantly renewing it' (RB_2: 110–11). Cf. **odu** and **tɔlodu**.

akaop |aka-op| (AKJ, NA) *n*

A boy or girl under certain ritual restrictions chiefly concerned with food

Attestations:

(1) <aka-op> 'person (...) under certain ritual restrictions, chiefly concerned with foods that may not be eaten' (RB_2: 94) (AKJ)

(2) <aka-op> 'a boy or girl [during the period of the initiation ceremonies]' (RB_2: 95), 'a youth or girl (...) who is abstaining from certain foods during the initiation period' (RB_2: 316) (NA)

Comparisons:

PGA *akaop* 'fasting person' (Abbi 2012: 328)

akapoŋ |aka-poŋ| (AKJ) *n*

Mouth

Attestations:

(1) <aka-poŋ> 'mouth' (RB_2: 23)

Comparisons:

PGA *akap^{h}oŋ* 'mouth' (Abbi 2012: 328); Akachari <tá póng> 'mouth' (*t-a-poŋ* 'my mouth') (Portman 1887: 51)

Notes:

Cf. **ɛrapoŋ** and **oŋpoŋ**.

akarka |aka-arka| (AKJ) *v*

To tell, to say

Attestations:

(1) <ak'-ar-ka> 'he says' [*sic*] (*akarka* |aka-arka| '(He) said') (RB_2: 24)

Comparisons:

PGA *akark^{h}a* 'to tell, to say' (Abbi 2013: 263, 322)

akatat |aka-tat| (AKJ) *n*

Tongue

Attestations:
(1) <âkà-tât> 'tongue' (M: 172)

Comparisons:
PGA *akaṭaṭ* 'tongue' (Abbi 2012: 328); Akachari <ákátát> 'id.' (Portman 1887: 85)

akaʧari |akaʧari| (NA) *n*
Akachari

Attestations:
(1) <aka-Čari-ar-bom> 'he talks the *Čari* language' (*aka-ʧari ar-bom* '(He) talks Akachari') (RB_2: 24)

Notes:
Cf. **ʧari**.

akaʧe |aka-ʧe| (NA) *v*
To accompany

Attestations:
(1) <ŋilio t-ače-bom> 'you (pl.) come with (accompany) me' (*ŋilio t=a-ʧe-bom* 'you (pl.) are accompanying me') (RB_2: 501), <ŋio t-ače-bom> 'you are coming with me' (*ŋio t=a-ʧe-bom* 'you (sg.) are accompanying me') (RB_2: 504)

Comparisons:
PGA *akaci* 'to come with, to follow someone' (Abbi 2013: 125, 242)

alebe (NA) *n*
Term of address for a girl during the initiation ceremony and for a short time afterwards

Attestations:
(1) <alebe> 'girl [during the initiation ceremony and for a short time afterwards]' (RB_2: 93)

Notes:
Synonym: **toto**.

ar (NA) *v*
To talk

Attestations:
(1) <aka-Čari-ar-bom> 'he talks the *Čari* language' (*aka-ʧari ar-bom* 'id.') (RB_2: 24)

arabela |ara-bela| (NA) *n*

Younger person of the same generation

Attestations:

(1) <ot-ara-bela> 'any person of the same generation who is younger' (*Ø-ot-ara-bela* 'his/her younger person of the same generation') (RB_2: 56)

Comparisons:

Cf. PGA *arabelo* 'younger sister' (Abbi 2012: 329)

Notes:

otarabela seems to be the possessed form of this kin term (see section 3.2.1.6).

araiʧulu |arai-ʧulu| (AKJ, NA) *adv*

After

Attestations:

(1) <arai-čulu> 'after' (RB_2: 500, 501) (AKJ)

(2) <arai-čulu> 'after, following, later in order' (RB_2: 499) (NA)

Comparisons:

PGA *rasulu* 'after that' (Abbi 2012: 381); Akachari <rá chulu> 'to follow' (Portman 1887: 33)

araiʧulute |arai-ʧulute| (AKJ, NA) *n*

Younger person of the same generation

Attestations:

(1) <ot-arai-čulute> 'he who was born after me' (RB_2: 66–7) (AKJ)

(2) <ot-arai-čulute> 'his younger brother' (*Ø-ot-arai-ʧulute* 'id.') (RB_2: 54), 'person younger than the speaker' (RB_2: 55), 'any person of the same generation who is younger' (RB_2: 56), 'younger person', 'he who was born after me' (RB_2: 66–7), <ŋ'ot-a-mai ot-arai-čulute> 'thy father's younger brother' (*ŋ-ot-a-mai Ø-ot-arai-ʧulute* 'id.') (RB_2: 56), <ot-e-bui ot-arai-čulute> 'his wife's younger brother' (*Ø-ot-e-bui Ø-ot-arai-ʧulute* 'id.') (RB_2: 56), <ot-arai-čulu-te> 'younger brother' (*Ø-ot-arai-ʧulute* 'his/her younger brother') (RB_2: 99) (NA)

Comparisons:

Cf. PGA *araʃuluʈhuo* 'younger sibling' (Abbi 2012: 330) and Akachari <ngára chulu tu> 'brother' and <ngárá chulutu> 'sister' (*ŋ-ara-ʧulutu* 'your (sg.) younger sibling') (Portman 1887: 19, 73)

Notes:

This term does 'not, strictly speaking, convey any idea of consanguinity, although [it is] commonly used to refer to a brother or a sister' (RB$_2$: 67). **otaraiʧulute** seems to be its possessed form (see section 3.2.1.6). 'Alternative words of the same meaning are *ot-ara-liču* and *ot-ara-bela*' (RB$_2$: 56); see **arabela** and **araliʧu**.

araiʧuluteʧip |arai-ʧulute-ʧip| (NA) *n*

Younger woman of the same generation

Attestations:

(1) <ot-arai-čulute-čip> 'his younger sister' (*Ø-ot-arai-ʧulute-ʧip* 'id.') (RB$_2$: 54)

araiʧulutu |arai-ʧulutu| (AKJ, NA) *v*

To follow

Attestations:

(1) <tio ŋ-arai-čulutu-bom> 'I follow thee' (*tio ŋ=arai-ʧulutu-bom* 'id.') (RB$_2$: 501) (AKJ)

(2) <tio ŋ'arai-čulutu-bom> 'I will follow you' (*tio ŋ=arai-ʧulutu-bom* 'id.') (RB$_2$: 55) (NA)

araket |ara-ket| (AKJ) *n*

Urine

Attestations:

(1) <arâ-kêt> 'urine' (M: 172)

araliʧu |ara-liʧu| (NA) *n*

Younger person of the same generation

Attestations:

(1) <ot-ara-liču> 'any person of the same generation who is younger' (*Ø-ot-ara-liʧu* 'his/her younger person of the same generation') (RB$_2$: 56)

Notes:

otaraliʧu seems to be the possessed form of this term (see section 3.2.1.6).

aramiku |ara-miku| (AKJ, NA) *n*

Space under

Attestations:

(1) <ara-miku> 'under' (RB$_2$: 500) (AKJ)

(2) <Tau'ra-miku> [place-name] (*tau-(a)ra-miku* 'space under the [*sic*] sky'; this toponym lacks the expected definite article *t*=) (RB$_2$: 227) (NA).

Comparisons:

Cf. PGA *imik*^{h}*u* 'inside' (Abbi 2013: 161)

Notes:

Cf. **ɛrmiku**, **maramiku** and **timiku**. Temple (1903: 31) records <Tàu-râ-míku> both as the local name of West Island, in Akachari territory, and of Excelsior Island, in Akakhora territory. In addition, he records <Tàu-tara-míku> (Temple 1903: 32), with the expected definite article *t*=, as the local name of Interview Island in Akakede territory.

araɲu |ara-ɲu| (NA) *n*

Village (possessed form?)

Attestations:

(1) <Lau t'ara-nyu> 'Penal Settlement [of Port Blair], the village of the spirits' (*lau t=Ø-ara-ɲu* 'village of the spirits') (RB$_2$: 137)

Comparisons:

PGA *ɲo* 'house, camp' (Abbi 2012: 374)

Notes:

See endnote 3 to Chapter 3.

atʃiu (AKJ) *pron*

Who

Attestations:

(1) <ačiu ŋ'a-mai bi?> 'Who your father is?' [*sic*] (*atʃiu ŋ-a-mai=bi* 'Who is your (sg.) father?') (RB$_2$: 54)

Comparisons:

PGA *aʃyu* 'who' (Abbi 2012: 330); Akachari <áchu> 'who' (Portman 1887: 109, 115)

balo (NA) *n*

Creeper

Attestations:

(1) <terkobito-balo> 'centipede creeper (*Pothos sandens*)' (RB$_2$: 99)

Comparisons:

PGA *balo* 'creeper' (Abbi 2012: 331)

bani (NA) *n*

Oriole

Attestations:

(1) <bani> 'the oriole' (RB_2: 118)

baraba (AKJ) *n*

Sleeping mat

Attestations:

(1) <baraba> 'a sleeping mat' (RB_1: 39), 'mat' (RB_2: 498)

Comparisons:

PGA *baraba* 'sleeping mat' (Abbi 2012: 332); Akachari <bárabá> 'id.' (Portman 1887: 209)

bat (NA) *n*

Night

Attestations:

(1) <Mimi Bat> 'Lady Night' (RB_2: 144)

Comparisons:

PGA *bat* 'night' (Abbi 2012: 332); Akachari <bát> 'id.' (Portman 1887: 53, 131, 189)

be (AKJ, NA) *n*

Mother-of-pearl shell

Attestations:

(1) <be> 'pearl shell' (RB_2: 198, 201) (AKJ)

(2) <be> 'pearl-shell' (RB_2: 165), 'mother-of-pearl shell, pearl shell' (RB_2: 368) (NA)

Comparisons:

PGA *bo* 'oyster' (Abbi 2012: 334); Akachari <be> 'pearl shell' (RB_2: 201)

beno (NA) *v*

To sleep

Attestations:

(1) <u-ben-om> 'someone sleeping, he sleeping' (*Ø-u beno-m* 'He/she is sleeping') (RB_2: 501), 'sleeping' (RB_2: 503), <n-u-ben-om> 'they sleeping' (*n-u beno-m* 'They are sleeping') (RB_2: 501), 'they (are) sleeping' (RB_2: 504), <u-beno-ba> 'he slept or was sleeping' (*Ø-u beno-ba* 'id.') (RB_2: 504)

Comparisons:
PGA *beno* 'sleep' (Abbi 2012: 332); Akachari <tubénó> 'to sleep' (*t-u beno* 'I am sleeping') (Portman 1887: 73)

beɲe (AKJ, NA) *n*
Bird sp.

Attestations:
(1) <benye> [a bird] (RB$_2$: 199) (AKJ)
(2) <benye> [a bird] (RB$_2$: 150) (NA)

beʧ (AKJ) *n*
Hair

Attestations:
(1) <(îr-)bê> [*sic*] 'hair (of head)' (M: 170)

Comparisons:
Cf. PGA *otbec* ~ *otbɛc* 'hair, body hair' (Abbi 2012: 376) and Akachari <paitch> 'id.' (Portman 1887: 37)

Notes:
Cf. **ɛrbeʧ** and **otbeʧ**. Man consistently gives the morpheme as <bê>, but RB$_2$ as well as the comparative material from PGA and Akachari suggest a final affricate; we therefore annotate all of Man's forms with the comment '[*sic*]'.

bɛrɛt (NA) *n*
Frog sp.

Attestations:
(1) <be̲re̲t> 'a smaller species of frog' (RB$_2$: 221–3)

Comparisons:
PGA *berɛt* ~ *bereːʈ* 'small frog' (Abbi 2012: 332)

=bi$_1$ (NA) *postp*
ABSOLUTIVE

Attestations:
(1) <tio bi tuŋ-om> 'I want (I am wanting)' (*tio=bi tuŋ-om* 'id.') (RB$_2$: 503), <Buio ǰo bi ewur-om> 'Buio is singing a song' (*buyo ʤo=bi e-ur-om* 'id.') (RB$_2$: 503), <io biwu bi moič-om> 'he is making a torch' (*io biu=bi moiʧ-om* 'id.') (RB$_2$: 504) (NA)

Comparisons:
PGA *-bi* 'absolutive' (Abbi 2012: 116–7); Akachari <-bé ~ -bí> [ABSOLUTIVE] (Portman 1887: 101–91, *passim*)

=bi$_2$ (AKJ, NA) *v*

To be

Attestations:

(1) <ačiu ŋ'a-mai bi?> 'Who your father is?' [*sic*] (*aʧiu ŋ-a-mai=bi* 'Who is your (sg.) father?') (RB_2: 54) (AKJ)

(2) <bi> [verbal particle] (M: 502), [particle] (M: 504), <Ino er-kimil bi> 'The water is hot' (*ino ɛr-kimil=bi*) (RB_2: 267), <kidi ko̲roin bi> 'this is a dugong' (*kidi kɔroin=bi* 'id.') (RB_2: 502), <kidi t-ičo bi> 'this is mine' (*kidi t-iʧo=bi* 'id.') (RB_2: 503), <deko b' era̲-lio> 'well! it is finished' (*deko b=ɛra-lio* '(It) is enough. (It) is finished') (RB_2: 503) (NA)

Comparisons:

PGA *bi* ~ *be* 'copula' (Abbi 2013: 240); Akachari <-bí ~ -bé> 'be' (Portman 1887: 95–191, *passim*)

bibi (NA) *n*

Dog

Attestations:

(1) <bibi> 'dog' (RB_1: 52)

Comparisons:

PGA *bibicao* 'bitch' (Abbi 2012: 333); Akachari <bíbí> 'dog' (Portman 1887: 27)

Notes:

<bibi poiye> 'dog not' (viz. 'There (were) not dogs') recorded by Radcliffe-Brown as a North Andamanese expression for indicating the times before Settlement of Port Blair (RB_1: 36) is specifically Akakede, as the negative particle <poiye> (<puíe> in Portman's Dialogues) reveals.

Man (1919–23: 50) indicates that '[t]his word — apparently of onomatopoeic origin — has been adopted since they [Man may be referring specifically to the Akabea, but the point applies *a fortiori* to ethnolinguistic groups living further from Port Blair — RZ/BC] became acquainted with dogs, about 1858'. It was also used in Akabea, Opuchikwar and Akakede (see Portman 1887: 26–7). The PGA form *bibicao* combines *bibi* with the name of the wild cat (*Paradoxurus Andamanensis*) recorded as <chāō> in Akachari (Portman 1887: 21).

bido (NA) *n*

Palm sp.: *Calamus tigrinus*

Attestations:

(1) <bido> '*Calamus tigrinus*' (RB_2: 136, 165), 'cane' (RB_2: 292)

Comparisons:

PGA *bid̪o* 'tree' (Abbi 2012: 332); Akachari <bétāū> 'Calamus' (Portman 1887: 217)

bido teʧ lau (NA) *n*

Spirit of the *Calamus* leaf

Attestations:

(1) <bido teč lau> 'spirit of the *Calamus* leaf' (RB_2: 136), <bido-teč lau> 'jungle spirit' (RB_2: 165), <bido-teč-lau> '*Calamus* leaf spirit' (RB_2: 292)

Notes:

Cf. **bido**, **lau** and **teʧ**.

biliku (AKJ, NA) *n*

1. A female supernatural being

Attestations:

(1) <Biliku> 'a mythical being' (RB_1: 40) 'mythical person' (RB_1: 51); cf also RB_2, pp. 197–9, 201, 206, 348 and 370 (AKJ)

(2) <Biliku> 'a mythical being' (RB_2: 141), 'a being' (RB_2: 145, 147, 163, 178), 'an anthropomorphic being' (RB_2: 377) (NA)

2. Spider

Attestations:

(1) <biliku> 'spider' (RB_2: 151, 156, 362) (NA)

Comparisons:

PGA *bilik^{h}u* 'God; spider' (Abbi 2012: 333); Akabo, Akakhora <Biliku> [a supernatural being] (RB_2: 147, 150, 199); Akachari <Biliku> (RB_2: 147, 150, 201), <bílek ke> [*sic*] 'God' (Portman 1887: 35)

Notes:

Biliku and her counterpart (commonly, her husband) **Tarai** (see below) are the personification of the north-east monsoon and the south-west monsoon respectively (RB_2: 353, 377). The North Andamanese believed that the transgression of certain taboos will infuriate Biliku to the point of sending stormy weather (RB_2: 163). She is often mentioned as the creator (or the mother) of sun and moon, the discoverer of fire and the inventor of netting and basketry

(RB_2: 150, 198, 201). Two beings with similar names were the most important supernatural entities also of the other Great Andamanese peoples. Their names are Puluga and Deria among the Akabea, Puluga and Daria among the Akarbale, Bilik and Teriye among the Opuchikwar, Bilak and Treyè among the Okol, Bilak and Treye among the Okojuwoi, Bilika and Tarai among the Akakede (Portman 1898: 68, 152–3 (Vocabulary); RB_2: 150–1). However, depending on the group, the second being was husband, wife, child, or friend of the first one (RB_2: 150–2). It is possible that the Akabea name *puluga* might be etymologically connected with the root *pulu* 'pour with water' (Portman 1898: 270). The Önge also have a supernatural female being identified with the north-east monsoon called by a similar name, *əluga* or *əluge*, which is also the term for 'monitor lizard' (<öluga>; RB_1: 51, RB_2: 151) and 'thunder' (recorded as <ölugé> by Portman (1887: 83), *eyuge* by Ganguly (1972: 9) and *əyuge* by Dasgupta and Sharma (1982: 97)). The name Önge *əluga*, *əluge*, *eyuge*, or *əyuge* is also parallel to Jarawa *oruːg* 'monitor lizard' (Sreenathan 2001: 100). We are therefore dealing with an Andamanese Wanderwort that probably spread into the languages of the Önge and Jarawa from Great Andaman (perhaps via Akabea).

biliku bɔto (lit. 'Biliku wind') (AKJ, NA) *n*

North-east wind

Attestations:

(1) <Biliku boto> 'N. E. Wind' (RB_2: 147) (AKJ)

(2) <Biliku b̲o̲to> 'the Biliku wind' (RB_2: 377) (NA)

Notes:

'(...) in the North Andaman *Biliku* and *Tarai* are used as the names of the two chief winds' (RB_2: 378).

biratkoro (NA) *n*

Bird sp.

Attestations:

(1) <biratkoro> [a bird] (RB_2: 150, 199)

biu (NA) *n*

K.o. resin

Attestations:

(1) <biwu> 'resin' (RB_2: 504), <io biwu bi moič-om> 'he is making a torch' (*io biu=bi moitʃ-om* 'id.') (RB_2: 504)

Comparisons:
PGA *biu* 'light; wood-smoke; incense' (Abbi 2012: 334); Akachari <bíu> 'resin' (Portman 1887: 217)

Notes:
The grapheme <w> of the original transcription of this word represents an epenthetic glide inserted in a two-vowel sequence of the type *Vu* (see section 2.1.1).

biumɔiʧ |biu-mɔiʧ| (NA) *n*
Torch of resin

Attestations:
(1) <biwu-mo̠ič> 'torch of resin' (RB_2: 504)

Comparisons:
PGA *biumoc* 'torch' (Abbi 2012: 334)

Notes:
Cf. **biu** and **mɔiʧ**.

bobelo (AKJ, NA) *n*
Bird sp.

Attestations:
(1) <bobelo> [a bird] (RB_2: 199) (AKJ)
(2) <bobelo> [a bird] (RB_2: 150) (NA)

bobi (NA) *n*
Creeper sp.

Attestations:
(1) <bobi> 'creeper' (RB_2: 465)

bol$_1$ (NA) *n*
Fish sp.

Attestations:
(1) <bol> 'a large eel' (RB_2: 217)

Comparisons:
PGA *bol* 'fish' (Abbi 2012: 334); Akabo <bol> 'fish found in inland creeks'

bol$_2$ (NA) *n*
Tree sp.: *Hibiscus tiliaceus*

Attestations:

(1) <bol> '*Hibiscus tiliaceus*' (RB_2: 118)

Comparisons:

PGA *bol* 'tree' (Abbi 2012: 334), *bole* '*Hibiscus tiliaceus* L.' (Awasthi 1991: 277)

bolok (AKJ, NA) *n*

Orphan

Attestations:

(1) <bolok> 'orphan' (RB_2: 112) (AKJ)
(2) <bolok> 'one who has lost a parent' (RB_2: 121) (NA)

Comparisons:

PGA *bolok* 'orphan' (Abbi 2012: 334)

boto (NA) *v*

To fall

Attestations:

(1) <t-u-boto-ba> 'I fell' (*t-u boto-ba* 'id.') (RB_2: 503), <u-boto-ba> 'he or it fell' (*Ø-u boto-ba* 'id.') (RB_2: 504)

Comparisons:

PGA *boṯo* 'fall' (Abbi 2012: 335); Akachari <tu bo tó> 'to fall' (*t-u boto* 'I am falling') (Portman 1887: 31)

bɔiʧo (NA) *v* (?)

To wrestle (?)

Attestations:

(1) <bo̲ičo> 'one who wrestles' (RB_2: 118)

Notes:

Recorded as a personal name, it could also be a verb (cf. **kiʤeri**).

bɔtek (AKJ) *n*

Plant sp.

Attestations:

(1) <bo̲tek> [flower-name] (RB_2: 119, 120)

bɔto (AKJ, NA) *n*

Wind

Attestations:

(1) <bo̲to> 'wind' (RB_2: 147, 193), <Biliku boto> 'N. E. Wind' (RB_2: 147), <Tarai boto> 'S. W. Wind' (RB_2: 147) (AKJ)

(2) <Biliku bo̲to> 'the Biliku wind' (RB$_2$: 377), <Tarai bo̲to> 'the Tarai wind' (RB$_2$: 377) (NA)

Comparisons:

PGA *bɔtɔ* 'storm' (Abbi 2012: 335); Akabo, Akachari, Akakhora <bo̲to> 'wind' (RB$_2$: 147) (cf. Akachari <bāūte> 'wind' in Portman (1887: 95))

bui (NA) *n*

K.o. vegetable food

Attestations:

(1) <bui> [a vegetable food] (RB$_2$: 199)

Comparisons:

PGA *bui* 'fruit' (Abbi 2012: 353); Akachari <bui> 'vegetable food' (RB$_2$: 96)

buku (NA) *adj*

Female

Attestations:

(1) <Lau-buku> 'spirit-women, female spirits' (*lau buku* 'id.') (RB$_2$: 291)

Comparisons:

PGA *buk*^{h}*u* 'female' (Abbi 2012: 335); Akachari <lāō buku> 'female' ('female spirit') (Portman 1887: 31), <lāōbuku> 'woman' (Portman 1887: 91)

Notes:

'(...) the natives of the North Andaman often use the expression *Lau-buku* (meaning literally "spirit-women" or "female spirits") to denote women collectively instead of the phrase that might be expected — *n'e-buku*. It would seem that by reason of their sex and the special ideas that are associated with it, women are regarded as having a very special relation with the world of spirits' (RB$_2$: 291). Cf. **ebuku**.

buliu (AKJ) *n*

Creek

Attestations:

(1) <Bo̲ro̲ŋ Buliu> [place name] (RB$_2$: 192)

Comparisons:

PGA *buliu* 'creek, canal, drain' (Abbi 2012: 335); Akabo <buliu> 'creek' (RB$_2$: 28); Akachari <bulíu> 'creek' (Portman 1887: 25, 105)

bun (AKJ, NA) *n*

Cyrena shell

Attestations:

(1) <bun> 'Cyrena shell used as knife' (RB_2: 498) (AKJ)

(2) <bun> 'Cyrena shell' (RB_2: 165) (NA)

Comparisons:

PGA *bun* 'shell' (Abbi 2012: 336); Akachari <bun> 'Cyrena-shell, used as a knife' (Portman 1887: 209)

burut (AKJ) *n*

Plant sp.

Attestations:

(1) <burut> [a plant] (RB_2: 183)

buyo (NA) *n*

Plant sp.: *Mucuna* sp.

Attestations:

(1) <buio> 'a species of *Mucuna*' (RB_2: 111), '*Mucuna sp.*, a plant with edible beans' (RB_2: 118)

Comparisons:

Akachari <bíu> 'Mucuna' (Portman 1887: 227)

deko (NA) *adj*

Enough

Attestations:

(1) <deko b' er<u>a</u>-lio> 'well! it is finished' (*deko b=ɛra-lio* '(It) is enough. (It) is finished') (RB_2: 503)

Comparisons:

PGA *ḍekʰo* 'now, enough' (Abbi 2012: 341)

deŋ (AKJ) *n*

Plant sp.

Attestations:

(1) <deŋ> [a plant] (RB_2: 183)

dik (NA) *n*

Prawn sp.

Attestations:

(1) <Maia Dik> 'Sir Prawn' (RB_2: 220)

Comparisons:
PGA *ḍik* 'prawn like creature' (Abbi 2012: 341); Akachari <Maia Dik> 'Sir Prawn' (RB$_2$: 189, 202)

diu (AKJ, NA) *n*
Sun

Attestations:
(1) <diu> 'sun' (RB$_2$: 498), <Mimi diu> 'sun' (lit. 'Lady Sun') (RB$_2$: 141) (AKJ)
(2) <diu> 'sun' (RB$_2$: 144) (NA)

Comparisons:
PGA *ḍiu* 'sun' (Abbi 2012: 341); Akachari <díu> 'id.' (Portman 1887: 79)

ʤekakɛt (?) (AKJ) *n*
Intestines, bowels

Attestations:
(1) <ǰekâ-kät> 'bowels (intestines)' (M: 169)

Notes:
This body part term is anomalous for two reasons: it does not seem to contain a somatic prefix; it has no known cognates in other Great Andamanese languages. In PGA, 'intestines, entrails' is *esudu* ~ *iʃuḍu* (Abbi 2012: 350, 360). Akachari has *eʧuḍu* 'belly, stomach' (cf. <échulu> 'belly' (Portman 1887: 15) and <méchudu> 'stomach' (lit. 'our stomach') (Portman 1887: 77)). These two forms are etymologically related to Akakede *iʧute*, Opuchikwar *abʧute*, Okol *oʧute*, Okojuwoi *aʧute*, Akabea *abʤodo* and Akarbale *abʤɔdo* 'belly, stomach, entrails'.

ʤeru (AKJ, NA) *n*
Tree sp.: *Sterculia* sp.

Attestations:
(1) <ǰeru> [flower-name] (RB$_2$: 119) (AKJ)
(2) <ǰeru> 'a species of *Sterculia*' (RB$_2$: 24, 311), [a plant] (RB$_2$: 93) (NA)

Comparisons:
PGA *ɟeru* 'flower' (Abbi 2012: 361)

Notes:
Cf. **akaʤeru**.

ʤi (AKJ) *n*

K.o. root

Attestations:

(1) <ǰi> 'edible root' (RB$_2$: 152)

ʤili (AKJ, NA) *n*

Plant sp.

Attestations:

(1) <ǰili> [flower-name] (RB$_2$: 119) (AKJ)
(2) <ǰili> [a plant] (RB$_2$: 93) (NA)

ʤin (AKJ) *n*

Plant sp.

Attestations:

(1) <ǰin> [a plant] (RB$_2$: 183)

Comparisons:

PGA *ɟin* 'tree' (Abbi 2012: 361)

ʤirmu (NA) *n*

A mythological animal that haunts the jungle

Attestations:

(1) <J̌irmu> 'a huge animal that haunts the jungle' (RB$_2$: 225)

Comparisons:

PGA *ɟirmu* 'mythic animal' (Abbi 2012: 361)

Notes:

'Throughout the Great Andaman there is a belief in a huge animal that haunts the jungles, or that haunted them in the days of the ancestors. In the North Andaman this beast is called *J̌irmu*. In the days of the ancestors it is supposed to have lived at *Ulibi-taŋ*, where it attacked and killed any men and women who came in its way. No detailed legend about *J̌irmu* was obtained' (RB$_2$: 225).

ʤiʧɛr (NA) *n*

Rain

Attestations:

(1) <ǰičer> 'rain' (RB$_2$: 145)

Comparisons:

PGA *ɟicɛr* 'rain' (Abbi 2012: 361); Akachari <jó chér> 'id.' (Portman 1887: 61)

ʤo$_1$ (AKJ, NA) *n*

Eating, food

Attestations:

(1) <ǰo> 'eating' (RB$_2$: 101) (AKJ)

(2) <ǰo> 'eating' (RB$_2$: 101, 267) (NA)

Comparisons:

PGA *ɟo* 'food' (Abbi 2012: 360); Akachari <aka jéo> [*sic*] 'food' (Portman 1887: 33)

ʤo$_2$ (NA) *n*

Song

Attestations:

(1) <Buio ǰo bi ewur-om> 'Buio is singing a song' (*buyo ʤo=bi e-ur-om* 'id.') (RB$_2$: 503)

Comparisons:

PGA *ɟo* 'song' (Abbi 2012: 361); Akachari <jóur> 'sing' (*ʤo ur* 'sing a song') (Portman 1887: 71), <jójur> 'song' (RB$_2$: 75), <jó> 'song' (RB$_2$: 109)

ʤurua (NA) *n*

Sea spirit

Attestations:

(1) <ǰurua> 'sea spirit' (RB$_2$: 136, 181), 'spirit of the sea' (RB$_2$: 157), 'spirit (…) inhabiting the sea' (RB$_2$: 163), [spirit] (RB$_2$: 140, 168, 374)

Comparisons:

PGA *ɟuruwaː* 'god' (Abbi 2012: 362); Akachari <ǰurua> 'spirit of a man's own country' (RB$_2$: 168).

Notes:

ʤuru is the South Andamanese (Akabea and Akarbale) term for 'sea', while a suffix *-wa* 'PERSON' is also found in South Andamanese.

ʤutpu (NA) *adj* (?)

Alone (?)

Attestations:

(1) <J̌utpu> [probably means] 'alone' (RB$_2$: 383)

Notes:

This is (also) the name of the first man on earth who 'made himself a wife from the nest of the white ant' (RB$_2$: 383).

ebui$_1$ |e-bui| (NA) *n*

Husband, wife

Attestations:

(1) <e-bui> 'his wife (her husband)' (*Ø-e-bui* 'id.') (RB$_2$: 54), <ot-e-bui> 'his wife (her husband)' (*Ø-ot-e-bui* 'id.') (RB$_2$: 54), <t'e-bui> 'my husband, my wife' (*t-e-bui* 'id.') (RB$_2$: 56), <t'ot-e-bui> 'my husband, my wife' (*t-ot-e-bui* 'id.') (RB$_2$: 56), 'husband, wife' (RB$_2$: 67), 'consort, the husband or wife of somebody' (RB$_2$: 500)

Comparisons:

PGA *eboe* 'husband, wife, spouse' (Abbi 2012: 343)

Notes:

otebui appears as a possessed form of this kin term (see section 3.2.1.6)

ebui otaraiʧulute |e-bui Ø-ot-arai-ʧulute| (lit. 'younger person of the same generation of the husband/wife') (NA)

Younger brother-in-law

Attestations:

(1) <ot-e-bui ot-arai-čulute> 'his wife's younger brother' (*Ø-ot-e-bui Ø-ot-arai-ʧulute* 'id.') (RB$_2$: 56)

Notes:

otebui otaraiʧulute appears as the possessed form of this kin expression (see section 3.2.1.6).

ebui$_2$ |e-bui| (NA) *v*

To marry, to be married

Attestations:

(1) <e-bui> 'marry' (RB$_2$: 499), <n'e-bui-om> 'they are married' (*n=e-bui-om* 'id.') (RB$_2$: 56)

Comparisons:

PGA *eboe* 'to marry' (Abbi 2013: 72); Akachari <ném boiyó> 'id.' (*n=e-m-boyo* 'They get married') (Portman 1887: 49)

ebuku |e-buku| (NA) *n*

Woman

Attestations:

(1) <e-buku> 'female' (RB$_2$: 499), <n'e-buku> 'women' (*n=e-buku* 'id.') (RB$_2$: 291)

Comparisons:

PGA *ibuxu* 'lady, female' (Abbi 2012: 358), *ebuk*^{h}*u* 'woman' (RB_2: 282); Akachari <ebuku> 'woman' (Portman 1887: 135), <ébuku> 'id.' (RB_2: 161, 167, 169), <ébukuí> 'id.' (RB_2: 173)

Notes:

Cf. **buku.**

eburɔŋo |e-burɔŋo| (AKJ) *n*

Side of the body

Attestations:

(1) <ê-bûrongo> 'chest' [*sic*] (M: 170), <ê-buròngo-tòi> 'rib' (*e-burɔŋo tɔi* 'bone of the side of the body') (M: 171) (AKJ)

Comparisons:

PGA *eburɔŋo* 'angle of a rib, side of the body' (Abbi 2012: 343)

eburoŋo tɔi |e-burɔŋo tɔi| (lit. 'bone of the side of the body') (AKJ)

Rib

Attestations:

(1) <ê-buròngo-tòi> 'rib' (M: 171) (AKJ)

edʒido |e-dʒido| (NA) *n*

A boy after his back was scarified in an initiation ceremony

Attestations:

(1) <ejido> [term of address] (RB_2: 95, 121, 295)

Comparisons:

PGA *eɟido* 'tattoo' (Abbi 2012: 344); Akachari <é jídó> 'to tattoo' (Portman 1887: 81)

Notes:

'When a boy, in the Northern tribes, has the scars made on his back, which show him to be no longer a child, his name is avoided for a few weeks and he is called *Ejido*' (RB_2: 121).

'At certain stages of the initiation ceremonies the name of a youth or of a girl (the flower-name in this instance) is avoided for a certain period. Such occasions are during, and for some time after, any of the more important ceremonies, such as the cutting of the boy's back, the puberty ceremony of the girl, the turtle-eating and pig-eating ceremonies. After a boy's back is cut he is addressed and spoken of for some time as *Ejido*, his own name not being spoken' (RB_2: 295).

Very probably, this word also means 'scarification' and/or 'to scarify'.

ele (AKJ) *n*
Lightning

Attestations:
(1) <ele> 'lightning' (RB_2: 145, 166, 367, 377)

Comparisons:
PGA *ale* 'lightning' (Abbi 2012: 328)

Notes:
Radcliffe-Brown also recorded a NA word <ale> 'lightning' (RB_2: 145), apparently identical to the PGA form. It could belong to a different NA dialect.

eleo |e-leo| (NA) *adj*
Small

Attestations:
(1) <e-leo> 'small' (RB_2: 499)

Comparisons:
PGA *eleo* 'small' (Abbi 2012: 345); Akachari <lāō> 'id.' (Portman 1887: 149, 171)

elobuŋ |e-lobuŋ| (AKJ) *adj*
Long, tall

Attestations:
(1) <e-lobuŋ> 'long, tall' (RB_2: 500)

Comparisons:
PGA *iloboŋ* 'long, tall' (Abbi 2012: 359); Akachari <é lóbung> 'tall' (Portman 1887: 81), <lóbung> 'long' (RB_2: 47)

Notes:
Used 'when referring to an object such as a canoe or a tree' (RB_2: 500). Cf. **ɛralobuŋ**.

elpe (NA) *v* (?)
To come and go (?)

Attestations:
(1) <elpe> 'one who comes and goes' (RB_2: 118)

Notes:
Recorded as a personal name, it could also be a verb (cf. **kiʤeri**).

empil |e-m-pil| (NA) *v*
To die

Attestations:

(1) <empilo> 'dead man' (*e-m-pil-o* 'died' (distant past)) (RB_2: 290); <em-pilo> 'dead' (RB_2: 499)

Comparisons:

PGA *empʰil* 'die' (Abbi 2012: 346); Akachari <em píl> 'id.' (Portman 1887: 27, 109, 149)

Notes:

<empilo> is a distant past verb form (cf. Abbi 2013: 234, 268), not a noun or an adjective as Radcliffe-Brown's translations might suggest.

enol |e-nol| (AKJ, NA) *adj*

Good

Attestations:

(1) <e-nol> 'good' (RB_2: 497) (AKJ)

(2) <kidi e-nol> 'this (is) good' (*kidi e-nol* 'id.') (RB_2: 504) (NA)

Comparisons:

PGA *enɔl* 'good' (Abbi 2012: 346); Akachari <nol> 'id.' (Portman 1887: 35, 158)

eŋet |e-ŋet| (AKJ) *n*

Navel

Attestations:

(1) <ing-it> 'navel' (M: 171)

Comparisons:

PGA *eŋet* 'navel' (Abbi 2012: 346); Akachari <méngét> 'id.' (*m-e-ŋet* 'our navel') (Portman 1887: 53)

epilu |e-pilu| (AKJ) *n*

Abdominal walls

Attestations:

(1) <ê-pilu> 'abdominal walls' (M: 169)

Comparisons:

PGA *epʰilu* 'belly' (Abbi 2013: 145)

epotaʧip |e-pota-ʧip| (NA) *n*

Mother-in-law

Attestations:

(1) <e-pota-čip> 'his mother-in-law' (*Ø-e-pota-ʧip* 'id.') (RB_2: 54), 'wife's mother, husband's mother' (RB_2: 56)

epotatʃiu |e-pota-tʃiu| (NA) *n*
Father-in-law

Attestations:
(1) <e-pota-čiu> 'his father-in-law' (*Ø-e-pota-tʃiu* 'id.') (RB$_2$: 54), 'wife's father, husband's father' (RB$_2$: 56)

etaru |e-taru| (NA) *n*
Man, male

Attestations:
(1) <e-taru> 'male' (RB$_2$: 499, 504)

Comparisons:
Akachari <é táru> 'man, male' (Portman 1887: 49)

Notes:
Cf. **taru**.

etei |e-tei| (NA) *n*
Fever

Attestations:
(1) <e-tei> 'fever' (RB$_2$: 499)

Comparisons:
PGA *ɛtei* 'fever, blood' (Abbi 2012: 356)

Notes:
Portman (1898: 346) indicates that when the Akabea 'are feverish, or have a headache, they often use the expression Ig-*té*-da meaning "Blood to the head", their idea being that the blood has heated and gone to the head'. Cf. **ɛratei**, **ottei** and **tei**.

etire$_1$ |e-tire| (NA) *adj*
New (of the moon)

Attestations:
(1) <dula e-tire> 'new moon' (*dula e-tire* 'id.') (RB$_2$: 143)

etire$_2$ |e-tire| (AKJ, NA) *n*
Child, offspring of an animal (non-possessed form)

Attestations:
(1) <e-tire> 'offspring' (RB$_2$: 124) (AKJ)
(2) <e-tire> 'child' (RB$_2$: 55, 499), 'offspring of an animal or of a human being' (RB$_2$: 68), 'young offspring of an animal or a

human being' (RB_2: 143, 499), <Bora e-tire> 'the child Bora' (*bora e-tire* 'Bora the child') (RB_2: 55), <e-tire Bora> 'the child Bora' (*e-tire bora* 'id.') (RB_2: 55) (NA)

Comparisons:

PGA *t*^{h}*ire* 'child' (Abbi 2012: 388); Akachari <étíré> 'baby' (Portman 1887: 15)

Notes:

This word is the non-possessed counterpart of **ottire**: 'The word *ot-tire* means "the child of somebody" without reference to any particular person as the parent' (RB_2: 68). Cf. **ɛratire** and **ottire**.

etomo |e-tomo| (AKJ) *n*

Flesh of the body, meat

Attestations:

(1) <e-tomo> 'muscle' (RB_2: 498), 'flesh or muscle of a human or animal body generally' (RB_2: 500), <e-tomo-t-ot-lam> 'muscularly powerful' (*Ø-e-tomo t=ot-lam* 'his/her flesh is strong') (RB_2: 498), 'muscle strong' (RB_2: 501)

Comparisons:

PGA *et*^{h}*omo* 'flesh, meat' (Abbi 2012: 351); Akachari <yetomó> 'flesh' (Portman 1887: 33), <yé tomo> 'meat' (Portman 1887: 49)

Notes:

Cf. **ɛratomo** and **tomo**.

eʧai |e-ʧai| (AKJ) *adj*

Bad

Attestations:

(1) <e-čai> 'bad' (RB_2: 498)

Comparisons:

PGA *cae* 'bad' (Abbi 2012: 336), *ecca:ye* 'id.' (Manoharan 1989: 113)

eʧɔ |e-ʧɔ| (AKJ) *n*

Lap, thigh

Attestations:

(1) <ê-chō-thômo> 'lap' (*e-ʧɔ tomo* 'flesh of the lap/thigh') (M: 171), <ê-chō-thōmo> 'thigh' (M: 172)

Comparisons:

PGA *ecɔpʈ*^{h}*omu* 'thigh' (Abbi 2012: 343)

eur |e-ur| (NA) *v*

To sing

Attestations:

(1) <Buio ǰo bi ewur-om> 'Buio is singing a song' (*buyo ʤo=bi e-ur-om* 'id.') (RB_2: 503)

Comparisons:

PGA *eure* 'sing' (Abbi 2012: 352); Akachari <jóur> 'id.' (*ʤo ur* '(He/she) sings a song') (Portman 1887: 71), <jójur> 'song' (Portman 1887: 75), <éwur> 'to sing' (Portman 1887: 109)

Notes:

The grapheme w> of the original transcription of this word represents an epenthetic glide inserted in two-vowel sequences of the type *Vu* (see section 2.1.1).

ɛrabat |ɛra-bat| (AKJ, NA) *n*

Tail (of snake or turtle)

Attestations:

(1) <o̲r-čubi t'e̲ra-bat> 'one customary pattern' (*ɔrtʃubi t=Ø-ɛra-bat* 'tail of the *Ophiophagus elaps* snake') (RB_2: 124) (AKJ)

(2) <or-čubi t'era-bat> 'design of zig-zag lines painted on the body with white clay' (RB_2: 484) (NA)

Comparisons:

PGA *era:bat̪* 'tail of the turtle' (Abbi 2012: 347)

ɛralio |ɛra-lio| (NA) *v*

To finish

<deko b' era̲-lio> 'well! it is finished' (*deko b=ɛra-lio* '(It) is enough. (It) is finished') (RB_2: 503)

Notes:

PGA *araliu* 'to finish' (Abbi 2013: 287), <jerá líwu> [*sic*] 'id.' (Portman 1887: 33).

ɛralobuŋ |ɛra-lobuŋ| (AKJ) *adj*

Long, tall

Attestations:

(1) <e̲ra-lobuŋ> 'long, tall' (RB_2: 500), <ti-t-e̲ra-lobuŋ> 'a long way' (*ti t=ɛra-lobuŋ* 'the long place') (RB_2: 500)

Comparisons:

PGA *lobɔŋ* 'long' (Abbi 2012: 369), *iloboŋ* 'long, tall'; Akachari <lóbung> 'long' (Portman 1887: 47), <é lóbung> 'tall' (RB_2: 81)

Notes:

Used 'when referring to distance between two points' (RB$_2$: 500). Cf. **elobuŋ**.

ɛrameo |ɛra-meo| (AKJ) *n*

Anchor

Attestations:

(1) <e̲ra-meo> 'anchor' (RB$_2$: 500)

Notes:

The Great Andamanese anchor is 'a heavy stone attached by rope to a canoe' (RB$_2$: 500). Cf. **meo**.

ɛrapoŋ |ɛra-poŋ| (AKJ, NA) *n*

Cave

Attestations:

(1) <Tarai-era-poŋ> 'the cave of Tarai' (*tarai Ø-ɛra-poŋ* 'id.') (RB$_2$: 192–3) (AKJ)

(2) <e̲ra-poŋ> 'cave' (RB$_2$: 160), <Pura-'ra-poŋ> [placename] (*pura Ø-(ɛ)ra-poŋ* 'cave of Pura (?)') (RB$_2$: 198) (NA)

Comparisons:

PGA *arap^{h}oŋ* 'cavity' (Abbi 2013: 155); Akachari <ára pong> 'to dig' (Portman 1887: 27), <rá pong> [*sic*] 'cave' (Portman 1887: 21), <póng> 'id.' (Portman 1887: 111, 115)

Notes:

The PGA noun phrases *ŋ-er-p^{h}ile t=Ø-ara-p^{h}oŋ* (2sg-SP-tooth DEF=3sg-SP-hole) 'your (sg,) dental cavity' and *t̪^{h}-er-kɔt̪^{h}o t=Ø-ara-p^{h}oŋ* (1sg-SP-nose DEF=3sg-hole) 'my nostrils' in Abbi (2013: 155) suggest that **ɛrapoŋ** denotes an anatomical cavity. The Akachari form <(a)rá pong> 'cave; to dig', on the other hand, suggests that this word was probably used also to refer to a naturally-occurring cavity formed underground. Cf. **akapoŋ** and **oŋpoŋ**.

ɛrapuli |ɛra-puli| (AKJ, NA) *n*

Pattern in painting a person ornamentally

Attestations:

(1) <e̲ra-puli> 'patterns' (RB$_2$: 122) (AKJ)

(2) <e̲ra-puli> 'patterns' (RB$_2$: 265, 269), 'designs' (RB$_2$: 265), <čokbi t'e̲ra-puli> 'turtle pattern' (*ʧokbi t=Ø-ɛra-puli* 'pattern of the turtle') (RB$_2$: 123), <ra t'e̲ra-puli> 'pig pattern' (*ra t=Ø-ɛra-puli* 'pattern of the pig') (RB$_2$: 123), <toto t'e̲ra-puli> 'pattern (...) used (...) to decorate a girl after the ceremony at

her first menstruation' (*toto t=Ø-ɛra-puli* 'pattern of the pandanus') (RB$_2$: 124), <kimil-t'e̲ra-puli> 'a pattern' (*kimil t=Ø-ɛra-puli* 'pattern of the boy or girl during the turtle-eating ceremony') (RB$_2$: 314) (NA)

Notes:

'These patterns are always made by the women, who decorate each other and their male relatives. The clay is mixed with water in a wooden dish or a shell and the mixture is applied to the body with the fingers. There is an almost indefinite variety in the patterns employed, although there are a certain number of what may be called usual designs' (RB$_2$: 122).

ɛratei |ɛra-tei| (AKJ) *n*

Menstruation

Attestations:

(1) <e̲ra-tei> 'menstruation' (RB$_2$: 500)

Comparisons:

PGA *ara:ttay* 'menses' (Abbi 2012: 330)

Notes:

Cf. **etei, ottei** and **tei.**

ɛratire |ɛra-tire| (AKJ, NA) *n*

Young shoot of a plant

Attestations:

(1) <e̲ra-tire> 'young shoots of a tree or plant' (RB$_2$: 500) (AKJ)

(2) <era-tire> 'offspring of a plant, the young shoots' (RB$_2$: 68) (NA)

Notes:

Cf. **etire** and **ottire.**

ɛratomo |ɛra-tomo| (AKJ) *n*

Buttocks

Attestations:

(1) <e̲ra-tomo> 'buttocks' (RB$_2$: 500), <era-thômo> 'id.' (M: 170)

Comparisons:

PGA *arat^{h}omo* 'buttocks; hips' (Abbi 2012: 330)

Notes:

Cf. **etomo** and **tomo.**

ɛrbala |ɛr-bala| (AKJ) *n*

Forearm

Attestations:

(1) <îr-bâla> 'fore-arm' (M: 169)

Comparisons:

PGA *ɛrbala* 'upper arm' (Abbi 2012: 354)

Notes:

The meaning seems to have shifted from 'forearm' to 'upper arm' in PGA.

ɛrbeʧ |ɛr-beʧ| (AKJ) *n*

Head hair

Attestations:

(1) <(îr-)bê> [*sic*] 'hair (of head)' (M: 170)

Comparisons:

Cf. PGA *otbec* ~ *otbɛc* 'hair, body hair' (Abbi 2012: 376) and Akachari <paitch> 'id.' (Portman 1887: 37)

Notes:

Cf. **beʧ** and **otbeʧ**.

ɛrboa |ɛr-boa| (AKJ) *n*

Lip

Attestations:

(1) <îr-bôa> 'mouth' (M: 171)

Comparisons:

PGA *erboa* 'lip; mouth' (Abbi 2012: 348); Akachari <ér buáh> 'lip' (Portman 1887: 47)

ɛrbuo |ɛr-buo| (AKJ) *n*

Ear

Attestations:

(1) <îr-bô> 'ear' (M: 170)

Comparisons:

PGA *erbuo* 'ear' (Abbi 2012: 348); Akachari <ér buáh> [*sic*] 'id.' (Portman 1887: 29)

ɛrkimil |ɛr-kimil| (NA) *adj*

Hot

Attestations:

(1) <er-kimil> 'hot' (RB$_2$: 101, 266), <Ino er-kimil bi> 'The water is hot' (*ino ɛr-kimil=bi* 'id.') (RB$_2$: 267)

Comparisons:

PGA *k*^{h}*imil* 'warm, hot' (Abbi 2012: 364); Akachari <kímil> 'hot' (Portman 1887: 39)

Notes:

Cf. **akakimil, kimil, kimilʤo, otkimil**$_1$ and **otkimil**$_2$.

ɛrkit |ɛr-kit| (AKJ) *n*

Arm

Attestations:

(1) <îr-kît> 'arm' (M: 169)

Comparisons:

PGA *erxi:ʈ* 'arm' (Abbi 2012: 350)

ɛrkɔto |ɛr-kɔto| (AKJ) *n*

Nose

Attestations:

(1) <îr-kâto> 'nose' (M: 171)

Comparisons:

PGA *erkɔʈ*^{h}*o* 'nose' (Abbi 2012: 349); Akachari <érkāū tó> 'nose' (Portman 1887: 169)

Notes:

<â>, used by Man for transcribing the open back vowel [ɑ:], might represent the open-mid back vowel [ɔ] or [ɔ:] in this word, as suggested by its PGA and Akachari equivalents.

ɛrkum |ɛr-kum| (AKJ) *n*

Shoulder

Attestations:

(1) <îr-kûm> 'shoulder' (M: 170)

Comparisons:

PGA *erk*^{h}*um* 'shoulder's edge' (Abbi 2013: 142)

ɛrkuro |ɛr-kuro| (NA) *adj*

Big

Attestations:

(1) <er-kuro> 'big' (RB$_2$: 45), <e̲r-kuro> 'big' (RB$_2$: 137), <ko̲roin t-er-kuro> 'a big dugong' (*kɔroin t=ɛr-kuro* 'the big dugong')

(RB_2: 504), <t-ičo roa t-er-kuro> 'my canoe is big' (*t-iʧo roa t=ɛr-kuro* 'id.') (RB_2: 504), <ra t'er-kuro> 'a big pig' (*ra t=ɛr-kuro* 'the big pig') (Radcliffe-Brown 1922: 496; not in RB_2) (NA)

Comparisons:
PGA *ɛrk^{h}uro* 'big, elder' (Abbi 2012: 355); Akachari <ér kura> [*sic*] 'big' (Portman 1887: 17)

ɛrmiku |ɛr-miku| (AKJ) *n*

1. Face

Attestations:
(1) <îr-mîko> [*sic*] 'face' (M: 171)

2. Forehead

Attestations:
(1) <îr-mîko> [*sic*] 'forehead' (M: 171)

Notes:
Cf. **aramiku**, **maramiku** and **timiku**.

ɛrnoko |ɛr-noko| (AKJ) *n*
Cheek

Attestations:
(1) <îr-nôko> 'cheek' (M: 170)

Comparisons:
PGA *ɛrnɔk^{h}o* 'cheek' (Abbi 2012: 355); Akachari <ér nóko> 'cheek' (Portman 1887: 21)

Notes:
<îr-nûku> 'lip' in M (p. 171) is probably an error for <îr-nôko> 'cheek'.

ɛrnoko beʧ |ɛr-noko beʧ| (lit. 'hair of the cheek') (AKJ)
Whiskers

Attestations:
(1) <īr-nôko-bê> [*sic*] 'whiskers' (M: 172)

ɛrpile |ɛr-pile| (AKJ) *n*
Tooth

Attestations:
(1) <îr-pilê> 'tooth' (M: 172)

Comparisons:
PGA *ɛrp^{h}ile* 'tooth' (Abbi 2012: 355); Akachari <mér pílé> 'tooth' (*m-er-pile* 'our teeth') (Portman 1887: 85)

ɛrtap |ɛr-tap| (AKJ) *n*

Lower jaw

Attestations:

(1) <îr-tap-bê> [*sic*] 'beard (jaw-hair)' (*ɛr-tap betʃ* 'hair of the lower jaw') (M: 169)

Comparisons:

PGA *ertap* 'lower jaw' (Abbi 2012: 349); Akachari <lāō tér táp> 'human jaw-bone ornament' (*lau t=Ø-er-tap* 'lower jaw of the spirit') (Portman 1887: 211)

ɛrtap betʃ |ɛr-tap betʃ| (lit. 'hair of the lower jaw') (AKJ)

Beard

Attestations:

(1) <îr-tap-bê> [*sic*] 'beard (jaw-hair)' (M: 169)

ɛrtʃar |ɛr-tʃar| (AKJ) *n*

Heart (seat of affections)

Attestations:

(1) <îr-châr> 'heart (seat of affections)' (M: 170)

Comparisons:

Cf. PGA *otcar* 'chest' (Abbi 2012: 377)

ɛrtʃo |ɛr-tʃo| (AKJ, NA) *n*

Head, skull

Attestations:

(1) <îr-chô> 'head' (M: 170) (AKJ)

(2) <e̱r-čo> 'head' (RB$_2$: 137), <lau t'e̱r-čo> 'skull [of a dead person]' (*lau t=Ø-ɛr-tʃo* 'skull of the dead person') (RB$_2$: 137) (NA)

Comparisons:

PGA *ɛrco* 'head, skull' (Abbi 2012: 354); Akachari <échu> 'head' (Portman 1887: 37), <érchu> 'skull' (RB$_2$: 169)

Notes:

Cf. **ottʃo**.

ɛrulu |ɛr-ulu| (AKJ) *n*

Eye

Attestations:

(1) <îr-ûlu> 'eye' (M: 170)

Comparisons:
PGA *erulu* 'eye' (Abbi 2012: 350); Akachari <ér ulu> 'id.' (Portman 1887: 29)

ɛrulu betʃ |ɛr-ulu betʃ| (lit. 'hair of the eye') (AKJ)
Eyebrow

Attestations:
(1) <îr-ûlu-bê> [*sic*] 'eye-brow' (M: 170)

ɛrulu totbetʃ |ɛr-ulu t=ot-betʃ| (lit. 'hair of the eye') (AKJ)
Eyelash

Attestations:
(1) <îr-ûlu-tû-bê> [*sic*] 'eye-lash' (M: 170)

Comparisons:
PGA *erulutobe:c* 'eyelash' (Abbi 2012: 83)

=il (NA) *postp*
LOCATIVE

Attestations:
(1) <il> 'in' (RB_2: 503), <čup il> 'in the basket' (RB_2: 503)

Comparisons:
PGA *=il* ~ *=el* ~ *=al* ~ *=l* 'locative' (Abbi 2013: 117, 127); Akachari *=il* ~ *=l* [id.] (Portman 1887: 15–211, *passim*)

ino (AKJ, NA) *n*

1. Water

Attestations:
(1) <ino> 'water' (RB_1: 40, 49; RB_2: 193)
(2) <Ino er-kimil bi> 'The water is hot' (*ino ɛr-kimil=bi* 'id.') (RB_2: 267)

2. Fresh water

Attestations:
(1) <ino ko̲lo to̲i> 'necklace of fresh-water shells' (lit. 'shells of a mollusc sp.') (RB_2: 480)

Comparisons:
PGA *ino* 'water' (Abbi 2012: 359); Akachari <ínó> 'id.'

ino kɔlo (AKJ) *n*
Mollusc sp.

Attestations:
(1) <ino ko̲lo to̲i> 'necklace of fresh-water shells' (RB_2: 480)

ino kɔlo tɔi (lit. 'shells of the mollusc of the fresh water') (AKJ)
Necklace of fresh-water shells

Attestations:
(1) <ino ko̲lo to̲i> 'necklace of fresh-water shells' (RB_2: 480)

Comparisons:
PGA *kolɔ* 'shell' (Abbi 2012: 365); Akachari <ínó kulāū> 'fresh-water shells' (Portman 1887: 211)

io |Ø-io| (AKJ, NA) *pron*
He, she, it

Attestations:
(1) <io> 'he, she, it' (RB_2: 501), <kule-l io> 'there is (it)' [*sic*] (*kulel io* 'It (is) there') (RB_2: 501) (AKJ)
(2) <io biwu bi moič-om> 'he is making a torch' (*io biu=bi moiʧ-om* 'id.') (RB_2: 504), <kule-l io> 'there is (it)' (NA)

Comparisons:
PGA *o* 'he, she, it' (Manoharan 1989: 68)

itpet |it-pet| (NA) *n*

1. Belly

Attestations:
(1) <it-pet> 'belly' (RB_2: 89)

2. Mother

Attestations:
(1) <Rea it-pet> '[Rea's] mother' (*rea Ø-it-pet* 'id.') (RB_2: 89)

Comparisons:
Cf. PGA *pɛṭ* 'to swell' (Abbi 2012: 379); Akachari <pet> 'belly' (RB_2: 189)

Notes:
Probably we are dealing with the possessed form of the term for 'belly' also used to refer to someone's mother.

iʧo |Ø-iʧo| (NA) *pron*
His, hers, her

Attestations:
(1) <ičo> 'belonging to' (RB_2: 66), [particle] (RB_2: 504), <Buio ičo roa> 'Buio's canoe' (*buyo Ø-iʧo roa*) (RB_2: 504) (NA)

Comparisons:
PGA *-ico* ~ *-iʃo* 'genitive' (Abbi 2013: 77, 99, 117, 130, 158, 163, 245)

kabal (NA) *n*

Mangrove sp.

Attestations:

(1) <kabal> 'a species of mangrove' (RB_2: 120)

Comparisons:

PGA *kabal* 'tree; seed' (Abbi 2012: 362); Akachari <kabal> 'mangrove fruit' (Portman 1887: 199)

=kak (NA) *postp*

ALLATIVE

Attestations:

(1) <kak> 'to (motion towards)' (RB_2: 503), <Lau-tiče kak> 'to Port Blair' (RB_2:)

Comparisons:

PGA *-ak* ~ *-a* 'directional' (Abbi 2012: 117, 126), *-ka:k* 'locative' (Manoharan 1989: 80); Akachari <-k> [allative] (Portman 1887: 123)

kataɲ (AKJ) *n*

1. Small star

Attestations:

(1) <katań> [small star] (RB_2: 141)

2. Firefly

Attestations:

(1) <katań> 'common fire-fly' (RB_2: 141)

Comparisons:

PGA *kaṭaɲ* 'star' (Abbi 2012: 363); Akachari <kátain> 'star' (Portman 1887: 77)

kea (NA) *v* (?)

To turn in one's sleep (?)

Attestations:

(1) <kea> 'one who turns in his sleep' (RB_2: 118)

Notes:

Recorded as a personal name, it could also be a verb (cf. **kiʤeri**).

keip (AKJ) *n*

A red pigment made by mixing burnt oxide of iron with animal or vegetable fat or oil

Attestations:

(1) <keyip> 'red oxide of iron' (RB_1: 39), 'a red pigment made by mixing burnt oxide of iron with animal or vegetable fat or oil' (RB_2: 122)

Comparisons:

PGA *keip* 'clay, red ochre' (Abbi 2012: 3); Akachari <kéip> 'red oxide of iron earth prepared' (Portman 1887: 213)

Notes:

The <y> with which this form was transcribed by Radcliffe-Brown likely represents an epenthetic [j]-glide (see 2.1.1).

kelil (AKJ, NA) *n*

Bird sp.

Attestations:

(1) <kelil> [a bird] (RB_2: 199) (AKJ)
(2) <kelil> [a bird] (RB_2: 150) (NA)

Comparisons:

Akakhora <kelil> [a bird] (Portman 1887: 199)

kidi (NA) *pron*

This

Attestations:

(1) <kidi t-ičo bi> 'this is mine' (*kidi t-itʃo=bi* 'id.') (RB_2: 503), <kidi k̲oroin bi> 'this is a dugong' (*kidi kɔroin=bi* 'id.') (RB_2: 502), <kidi e-nol> 'this (is) good' (*kidi e-nol* 'id.') (RB_2: 504) (NA)

Comparisons:

PGA *kʰidi* 'this (proximate, very close)' (Abbi 2012: 364); Akachari <kídí> 'this' (Portman 1887: 115, 119, 155, 157, 167, 179)

kidʒeri (NA) *v*

To walk backwards and forwards, to wander

Attestations:

(1) <kiǰe̲ri> 'one who walks backwards and forwards' (RB_2: 118)

Comparisons:

PGA *kiɟire* 'to wander, to roam around' (Abbi 2012: 364)

Notes:

This is also a personal name.

kimil (AKJ, NA) *n*

1. A brief period of unsettled weather at the end of the rainy season

Attestations:

(1) <kimil> 'a brief period of unsettled weather' (RB_2: 39), 'the latter part of the rainy season' (RB_2: 267), 'a particular season of the year' (RB_2: 308), 'period of six or eight weeks in which the weather is unsettled' (RB_2: 352), 'season (October and November)' (RB_2: 358) (NA)

(2) <kimil> 'season of storms' (RB_2: 153) (AKJ)

2. A boy or girl during the turtle-eating ceremony (**kimilʤo ʧokbi kimil**) or the pig-eating ceremony (after which the boy or girl is again free to eat pork) and for some months afterwards

Attestations:

(1) <kimil> [term of address] (RB_2: 101, 121, 295), <kimil-t'e̲ra-puli> 'a pattern' (*kimil t=Ø-ɛra-puli* 'pattern of the boy or girl during the turtle-eating ceremony') (RB_2: 314) (NA)

Comparisons:

PGA *kʰimil* 'warm, hot' (Abbi 2012: 364): Akachari <kímil> 'rainy season' (Portman 1887: 63, 97)

Notes:

kimil is the same root occurring in **ɛrkimil** 'hot' and **otkimil**$_1$ 'id.'. Radcliffe-Brown observes that '[t]he word "hot" is used by the natives in several unusual ways when they are talking their own language or Hindustani. Thus a stormy or rough sea is said to be "hot," and one native in describing to me (in Hindustani) the cessation of a cyclone said "the sea become cold." A person who is ill is said to be hot, and getting well is expressed by the phrase "getting cool."' (RB_2: 267). We can say that **kimil** 'denotes a condition of social danger, or of contact with power possessed by all things that can affect the life and safety of the society. It is obviously in this sense, and not as meaning "hot," that it is applied to the season in question, for the months of October and November are fairly cool, certainly very much cooler that February and March' (RB_2: 352).

Notes:

Cf. **akakimil, ɛrkimil, kimilʤo, otkimil**$_1$ and **otkimil**$_2$.

kimil tɛrapuli |kimil t=Ø-ɛra-puli| (lit. 'pattern of the boy or girl during the turtle-eating ceremony') (NA)

Pattern used to decorate a boy or a girl after the initiation ceremony

Attestations:

(1) <kimil-t'e̲ra-puli> 'a pattern' (RB$_2$: 314)

Notes:

'After the ceremony is over the initiate is painted with clay in a pattern called *kimil-t'e̲ra-puli* which consists of a background of the clay on which a pattern of separate spirals is made with the finger' (RB$_2$: 314).

kimilʤo (NA) *n*

Turtle-eating ceremony

Attestations:

(1) <kimil-ǰo> 'turtle-eating ceremony' (RB$_2$: 101, 267)

Comparisons:

PGA *k*^{h}*imilɟo* 'turtle-eating ceremony' (Abbi 2012: 364)

Notes:

Cf. **akakimil, ʤo, ɛrkimil, kimil, otkimil**$_1$ and **otkimil**$_2$.

=ko (NA) *postp*

INESSIVE (?)

Attestations:

(1) <ko> 'in or at a place' (RB$_2$: 503), <ŋ-oŋ-ko̲ro ko> 'in thy hand' (*ŋ-oŋ-kɔro=ko* 'id.') (RB$_2$: 503)

Notes:

Distinct from the locative =*il*; no known cognates in other GA languages.

koloko (NA) *part* (?)

COLLECTIVE (for human nouns)

Attestations:

(1) <koloko> 'people' (RB$_2$: 28, 190), <n'a-mai-koloko> 'ancestors' (*n=a-mai-koloko* 'id.') (RB$_2$: 190)

Comparisons:

PGA *kɔ:rlɔxo* [human noun plural marker] (Manoharan 1989: 61), *t*^{h}*irɛ kɔ:rlɔxo* 'children' (Abbi 2012: 388); Akabo <koloko> [people] (RB$_2$: 190)

Notes:

kɔ:rlɔxo is described by Manoharan as a 'bound morpheme to the common human nouns', though his transcription and that of Abbi in Abbi (2012) suggest a separate word. Supposing that it is an independent word, we assign **koloko**, together with **pu**, to the residual word class of particles (4.18).

komar (AKJ, NA) *n*

Fish sp.

Attestations:

(1) <komar> 'a species of fish' (RB_2: 101), [a fish] (RB_2: 112) (AKJ)

(2) <komar> 'fish' (RB_2: 89, 269)

Comparisons:

PGA *komar* 'a kind of sea fish' (Abbi 2012: 365); Akachari <komar> 'a fish' (RB_2: 96), <kumár> [a fish] (Portman 1887: 201)

korotli (AKJ) *n*

Creeper sp.

Attestations:

(1) <korotli> 'a creeper' (RB_2: 183)

korude (NA) *n*

Thunder

Attestations:

(1) <korude> 'thunder' (RB_2: 145, 367), <korule> 'id.' (RB_2: 145)

Comparisons:

PGA *kuruḍe* 'thunder' (Abbi 2012: 368)

Notes:

Radcliffe-Brown's representation of the last consonant of this word both with <d> and <l> suggests it is a retroflex sound.

kɔbo (AKJ, NA) *n*

1. Palm sp.: *Licuala* sp.

Attestations:

(1) <ko̲bo> 'Licuala palm' (RB_1: 39) (AKJ)

(2) <ko̲bo> *'Licuala"* (RB_2: 218) (NA)

2. Palm leaf (*Licuala* sp.)

Attestations:

(1) <ko̲bo> 'large palm leaves' (RB_2: 106) (AKJ)

Comparisons:

PGA *kɔbo* 'palm leaf' (Abbi 2012: 366)

kɔlo (AKJ, NA) *n*

Sea-eagle

Attestations:

(1) <ko̱lo> [a bird] (RB$_2$: 150, 199), <Maia Ko̱lo> 'Sir Sea-eagle' (RB$_2$: 207) (AKJ)

(2) <ko̱lo> 'sea-eagle' (RB$_2$: 227), <Maia Ko̱lo> 'Sir Sea-eagle' (RB$_2$: 227) (NA)

Comparisons:

PGA *kɔlɔ* 'brahminy kite, *Haliastur indus*' (Pande and Abbi 2011: 7), 'kite' (Abbi 2012: 366)

kɔnmo (NA) *n*

Yam sp.: *Dioscorea* sp.

Attestations:

(1) <ko̱nmo> '*Dioscorea* sp.' (RB$_2$: 118, 220), 'a species of *Dioscorea*' (RB$_2$: 198), [a vegetable food] (RB$_2$: 199)

Comparisons:

PGA *kɔnmo* 'potato; white tuber' (Abbi 2012: 366); Akachari <ko̱nmo> 'yam' (RB$_2$: 189, 202), <kāūnmu> 'id.' (Portman 1887: 91)

kɔro (AKJ, NA) *n*

Shredded palm-leaf fibre

Attestations:

(1) <koro> 'shredded palm-leaf stem' (RB$_2$: 108), <ko̱ro> 'material [obtained from the leaf-stem of a species of palm]' (RB$_2$: 453), 'fibre' (RB$_2$: 479) (AKJ)

(2) <koro> 'shredded palm-leaf stem' (RB$_2$: 127, 134, 139), <ko̱ro> 'shredded palm-leaf fibre' (RB$_2$: 177), 'shredded fibre' (RB$_2$: 290), 'fibre' (RB$_2$: 291, 292) (NA)

Comparisons:

PGA *kɔrɔ* 'green cane leaf' (Abbi 2012: 367)

kɔrotʃop |kɔro-tʃop| (NA) *n*

Structure erected across a dancing ground

Attestations:

(1) <koro-čop> (RB$_2$: 134)

Notes:

'In the village of this group [the group that made the last attack on another group – RZ/BC] the dancing ground is prepared, and across it is erected what is called a *koro-čop*. Posts are put up in a line, to the tops of these is attached a length of strong cane, and from the cane are suspended bundles of shredded palm-leaf (*koro*)' (RB$_2$: 134). Cf. **kɔro** and **ʧop**.

kɔroin (NA) *n*

Dugong

Attestations:

(1) <kidi ko̲roin bi> 'this is a dugong' (*kidi kɔroin=bi* 'id.') (RB$_2$: 502), <ko̲roin t-er-kuro> 'a big dugong' (*kɔroin t=ɛr-kuro* 'the big dugong') (RB$_2$: 504)

Comparisons:

PGA *kɔrɔiɲ* 'dugong' (Abbi 2012: 367); Akachari <kóroin> 'id.' (Portman 1887: 29, 145)

kɔrɔin (AKJ) *n*

Tree sp.: *Dipterocarpus laevis.*

Attestations:

(1) <koroin> 'Dipterocarpus tree' (RB$_1$: 39), <ko̲ro̲in> 'Dipterocarpus' (RB$_2$: 497)

Comparisons:

PGA *kɔrɔiɲ* 'Gurjan tree' (Abbi 2012: 367); Akachari <kāūroin> 'Dipterocarpus lævis (*Gorjon*)' (Portman 1887: 217)

kɔt (AKJ) *n*

Nest of the white ants

Attestations:

(1) <ko̲t> 'nest of the white ants', 'ant's [*sic*] nest' (RB$_2$: 192)

Comparisons:

PGA *kɔʈoʈco* 'mound of white ants' (Abbi 2012: 367)

kudu (AKJ) *n*

K.o. belt of pandanus leaves worn by girls and women

Attestations:

(1) <kudu> 'a belt' (RB$_2$: 477)

Comparisons:

Akachari <kudu> 'belt (broad and flat)' (Portman 1887: 209)

Notes:

'A belt is made in much the same way [as the **toto tɛrbua** – RZ/BC] out of *Pandanus* leaves split in half down the midrib, giving strips of about 2.5 cm. broad. Such belts have only a scanty tassel of thin strips of leaf at the back. They are worn by girls and women only' (RB_2: 477).

kulel (AKJ, NA) *adv*

There (distant)

Attestations:

(1) <kule-l io> 'there is (it)' [*sic*] (*kulel io* 'It (is) there') (RB_2: 501) (AKJ)

(2) <kule-l io> 'there is (it)' [*sic*] (RB_2: 504) (NA)

Comparisons:

PGA k^{h}*ulol* 'there (distant)' (Abbi 2012: 368); Akachari <kulol> 'there' (Portman 1887: 105)

kutobi (AKJ) *n*

1. Netting needle

Attestations:

(1) <kutobi> 'a netting needle' (RB_1: 39)

2. Reel used in rope-making

Attestations:

(1) <kutobi> 'reel' (RB_2: 453)

Comparisons:

Akachari <kutāūbí> 'netting needles for small nets' (Portman 1887: 207)

Notes:

'In rope-making the *Hibiscus* or other fibre (*Sterculia* or *Grewia*) is taken and twisted into a long strand, either with the fingers, or on the thigh by rolling beneath the palm of the hand, short lengths of fibre being added until a single twisted strand of sufficient length and uniform thickness is produced. The middle of this strand is passed over a piece of wood held by the toes, one half of it being wound on to a reel (*kutobi* in Aka-Jeru) made by tying together crossways two pieces of cane or wood each about 20 cm. long and 6 mm. in diameter' (RB_2: 455).

labo (AKJ) *n*

K.o. root

Attestations:

(1) <labo> 'edible root' (RB_2: 152)

Comparisons:
PGA *labo* 'root, tuber' (Abbi 2012: 368); Akachari <labo> 'edible root' (RB$_2$: 96)

laro (AKJ) *n*

Tree sp.: *Erythrina orientalis*

Attestations:

(1) <laro> 'a tree' (RB$_2$: 183)

Comparisons:
PGA *laro* '*Erythrina orientalis* (L.) Merr.' (Awasthi 1991: 277)

lau (NA) *n*

1. Spirit

Attestations:

(1) <lau> 'spirit' (RB$_2$: 136, 137, 145, 163, 167–9, 173, 176, 289, 290, 334, 373), 'spirit of the dead' (RB$_2$: 285), [spirit] (RB$_2$: 374), <lau tei> 'spirit blood' (*lau tei* 'id.') (RB$_2$: 119), <Lau-buku> 'spirit-women, female spirits' (*lau buku* 'id.') (RB$_2$: 291)

2. Light-skinned person (European or Asian)

Attestations:

(1) <lau> 'European' (RB$_2$: 137), [light-skinned alien] (RB$_2$: 138)

Comparisons:
PGA *lao* 'ghost, spirit; outsider, stranger, foreigner' (Abbi 2012: 368); Akachari <lāō> 'Indian' (Portman 1887: 41), 'convict' (Portman 1887: 111)

Notes:
Lau denotes a spirit 'inhabiting the forest' (RB$_2$: 163). 'The name *Lau* (...) is also applied by the Andamanese to the natives of India and Burma whom they see in the Penal Settlement of Port Blair' (RB$_2$: 137). 'Natives of the North Andaman told me that in former times (before 1875) they applied the term *Lau* to Europeans and not distinguishing them from other light-skinned aliens' (RB$_2$: 137).

lau taraɲu |lau t=Ø-ara-ɲu| (lit. 'village of the spirits') (AKJ)
Port Blair

Attestations:

(2) <Lau t'ara-nyu> 'Penal Settlement [of Port Blair], the village of the spirits' (RB$_2$: 137)

lau tɛrkuro |lau t=ɛr-kuro| (lit. 'the big spirit') (NA)
Ancestor

Attestations:
(2) <Lau t'e̱r-kuro> 'mythical ancestor' (RB_2: 137), <Lau t'er-kuro> 'ancestor' (RB_2: 190)

lau tɛrʧo |lau t=Ø-ɛr-ʧo| (lit. 'head of the dead person') (NA)
Skull of a dead person

Attestations:
(2) <Lau t'e̱r-čo> 'skull [of a dead person]' (RB_2: 137)

lau tɔi (lit. 'bone of the spirit') (NA)
Bone of a dead person

Attestations:
(2) <Lau to̱i> 'bones of a dead person' (RB_2: 137, 301)

lautiʧe (NA) *n*
Port Blair

Attestations:
(2) <Lau-tiče kak> 'to Port Blair' (RB_2: 503)

Notes:
The initial *lau* is the term for 'spirit, light-skinned person' (cf. **lau taraɲu**). The analysis and meaning of <tiče> are obscure.

lirʧitmo (AKJ) *n*
Kingfisher sp.

Attestations:
(2) <Maia Lirčitmo> 'Sir Kingfisher' (RB_2: 201)

lɔito (AKJ) *n*
K.o. root

Attestations:
(2) <lo̱ito> [an edible root] (RB_2: 52)

Comparisons:
Akakhora <lo̱ito> [a root] (RB_2: 199); Akachari <lo̱ito> [a vegetable food] (RB_2: 96)

luremo (NA) *n*
Rope

Attestations:
(2) <luremo> 'rope' (RB_2: 118)

Comparisons:
PGA *luremo* 'rope' (Abbi 2012: 369); Akachari <lurémo> 'id.' (Portman 1887: 65)

m= (NA) *pron*
We

Attestations:
(2) <m-> 'we' (RB_2: 501)
PGA *m=* '1pl' (Abbi 2013: 174); Akachari <m-> 'we' (Portman 1887: 123)

mai (AKJ, NA) *n*
Sir, mister

Attestations:
(1) <Mai> 'Sir' (RB_2: 65) (AKJ)
(2) <Mai> 'Sir' (RB_2: 44), <Mai Bora> 'Sir Bora' (RB_2: 44) (NA)

Notes:
Variant: **maya**. Cf **akamai**.

maramiku |m-ara-miku| (NA) *n*
World of the spirits that lies under this one

Attestations:
(1) <Maramiku> 'world that lies under this one' (RB_2: 168)

Notes:
Lit. 'our space under'. 'This world of spirits is said to be just like the actual world, with forest and sea, and all the familiar animal and vegetable species. The inhabitants spend their time just as the Andamanese do on earth, hunting, fishing and dancing' (RB_2: 168). Cf. **aramiku**, **ɛrmiku** and **timiku**.

maro (NA) *n*
Black honey

Attestations:
(1) <maro> 'honey' (RB_2: 118)

Comparisons:
PGA *maro* 'honeybee' (Abbi 2012: 370); Akachari <máró> 'black honey' (Portman 1887: 155, 197)

Notes:
Probably, *maro* is also the name of the black bee; cf. Akachari <máro béich> 'black bees' wax' (Portman 1887: 215).

maya (AKJ, NA) *n*

Sir, mister

Attestations:

(1) <Maia> 'a term of address' (RB$_1$: 40), 'Sir' (RB$_2$: 65), <Maia J̌utpu> [a legendary ancestor] (RB$_1$: 45) , <tičo maia> 'my father' (*t-itʃo maya* 'id.') (RB$_1$: 66), <Maia Čirikli> 'moon' (lit. 'Sir Moon') (RB$_1$: 141), <Maia Čoinyop> [a man] (RB$_1$: 142), <Maia Lirčitmo> 'Sir Kingfisher' (RB$_1$: 201) (AKJ)

(2) <Maia Tiritmo> 'Sir Kingfisher' (RB$_2$: 201) (AKJ (?))

(3) <Maia> 'Sir' (RB$_2$: 44, 53, 191), <Maia Bora> 'Mr Bora, Sir Bora' (RB$_2$: 54), <Maia Tok> [the husband of the moon] (RB$_2$: 141), <Maia Buio> [a man] (RB$_2$: 121), <Maia Kaba> [a man] (RB$_2$: 121), <Maia Ele> 'thunder' [*sic*] (lit. 'Sir Lightning') (RB$_2$: 145), <Maia Tarai> [Sir Tarai] (RB$_2$: 150), <Maia Tiritmo> 'Sir Kingfisher' (RB$_2$: 201), <Maia Mo̱ičo> 'Sir Rail' (RB$_2$: 220), <Maia Taolu> [Sir Taolu] (RB$_2$: 345) (NA)

Comparisons:

PGA *maya* 'deceased (used for forefathers)' (Abbi 2012: 370); Akachari <Maia> 'Sir' (RB$_2$: 189), <Maia Dula> [Sir Moon] (RB$_2$: 141), <Maia Dik> 'Sir Prawn' (RB$_2$: 207)

Notes:

Variant: **mai**. The noun phrase <tičo maia> is presumably grammatically correct, but was not used to express 'my father'. As Radcliffe-Brown notes, '[in] *Aka-J̌eru* a man speaks of his father as *t'a-mai*' (RB$_2$: 66).

meo (AKJ, NA) *n*

Stone

Attestations:

(1) <meo> 'stone' (RB$_2$: 500) (AKJ)

(2) <meo> 'stone' (RB$_2$: 118) (NA)

Comparisons:

PGA *meɔ* 'stone; glass' (Abbi 2012: 371); Akachari <méāū> 'stone' (Portman 1887: 77)

Notes:

Cf. **ɛrameo**.

mikulu (AKJ) *n*

K.o. root

Attestations:

(1) <mikulu> 'edible root' (RB_2: 152)

Comparisons:

PGA *mikulu* 'edible root' (Abbi 2012: 371); Akachari <mikulu> 'edible root' (RB_2: 96), <míkoló> 'root' (Portman 1887: 199); Akakhora <mikulu> [a root] (RB_2: 199)

milidu (AKJ, NA) *n*

Bird sp.

Attestations:

(1) <milidu> [a bird] (RB_2: 199) (AKJ)
(2) <milidu> [a bird] (RB_2: 150) (NA)

Comparisons:

PGA *miliḏu* 'Nicobar pigeon, *Caloenas nicobarica*' (Pande and Abbi 2011: 37), 'pigeon' (Abbi 2012: 371)

milite (NA) *n*

Mist

Attestations:

(1) <milite> 'mist' (RB_2: 145)

Comparisons:

PGA *biliṯe* 'mist' (Abbi 2012: 333)

mimi (AKJ, NA) *n*

Lady

Attestations:

(1) <mimi> 'Lady' (RB_2: 133), <Mimi Biliku> [Lady Biliku] (RB_2: 45, 141), <Mimi Čara> [Lady Čara] (RB_2: 206), <Mimi Kota> [Lady Kota] (RB_2: 206) (AKJ)
(2) <Mimi> [term of address] (RB_2: 54), 'Lady' (RB_2: 65, 191), [Lady] (RB_2: 70, 141), <Mimi Kaba> [Lady Kaba] (RB_2: 45), <Mimi Biliku> [Lady Biliku] (RB_2: 121, 150), <Mimi Diu> [Lady Sun] (RB_2: 141), <Mimi Bat> [Lady Night] (RB_2: 144, 377), <Mimi Ele> [Lady Lightning] (RB_2: 145), <Mimi Mo̱ičo> 'Lady Rail' (RB_2: 221) (NA)

Comparisons:

PGA *mimi* 'elderly lady, madam' (Abbi 2012: 371)

Notes:

Cf. **akamimi**.

mino (NA) *n*

Yam sp.: *Dioscorea* sp.

Attestations:

(1) <mino> 'a species of *Dioscorea*' (RB_2: 198), [a vegetable food] (RB_2: 199), '*Dioscorea* sp.' (RB_2: 220)

Comparisons:

PGA *mino* 'tuber; potato' (Abbi 2012: 371); Akachari <mino> 'edible root' (RB_2: 96), <mímó> 'yam' (Portman 1887: 91)

mio |m-io| (AKJ) *pron*

We

Attestations:

(1) <mio> [personal pronoun] (RB_2: 501) (AKJ)

Comparisons:

PGA *mio* 'we' (Abbi 2012: 306); Akachari <míó> 'id.' (Portman 1887: 89)

mirid (AKJ) *n*

Imperial pigeon

Attestations:

(1) <mirid> 'the Imperial pigeon' (RB_1: 39, 52)

Comparisons:

PGA *merit* 'blue rock pigeon, *Columba livia*' (Pande and Abbi 2011: 35), *mirit* 'bird' (Abbi 2012: 371); Akachari <mírid> 'pigeon' (Portman 1887: 57)

mit (AKJ) *n*

Plant sp.

Attestations:

(1) <mit> [a plant] (RB_2: 183)

mite$_1$ (AKJ) *n*

Bird sp.

Attestations:

(1) <mite> [a bird] (RB_2: 199)

Comparisons:

PGA *mit*^{h}*e* 'Andaman cuckoo-dove, *Macropygia rufipennis andamanica*' (Pande and Abbi 2011: 33), *mitɛ* 'bird' (Abbi 2012: 371); Akachari <mite> 'bronze-winged dove' (Portman 1887: 201), <Maia Mite> 'Sir Dove' (RB_2: 189, 202, 207)

mite$_2$ (AKJ, NA) *n*

Cicada

Attestations:

(1) <mite> 'cicada' (RB$_2$: 206) (AKJ)

(2) <mite> 'cicada' (RB$_2$: 150, 154, 198) (NA)

moiʧ (NA) *v*

To make a torch of

Attestations:

(1) <io biwu bi moič-om> 'he is making a torch' (*io biu=bi moiʧ-om* 'He is making a torch of resin') (RB$_2$: 504)

mɔiʧo (AKJ, NA) *n*

Rail

Attestations:

(1) <Mo̲ičo> 'rail' (RB$_2$: 202) (AKJ)

(2) <Maia Mo̲ičo> 'Sir Rail' (RB$_2$: 220), <Mimi Mo̲ičo> 'Lady Rail' (RB$_2$: 221) (NA)

Comparisons:

PGA *mɔcɔ* ~ *moco* 'domestic cock' (Pande and Abbi 2011: 14), *mɔcɔ* 'rooster' (Abbi 2012: 372); Akachari <moicha> 'fowl' (Portman 1887: 35)

mɔyo (AKJ) *n*

Tree sp.: *Sterculia* sp.

Attestations:

(1) <mo̲io> 'Sterculia tree' (RB$_1$: 39)

Comparisons:

Akachari <moiyó> 'Sterculia (*Auk yenzà*)' (Portman 1887: 225)

mukui (AKJ) *n*

Plant sp.

Attestations:

(1) <mukui> [flower-name] (RB$_2$: 119)

n= (NA) *pron*

They

Attestations:

(1) <n-> (RB$_2$: 501), <n'e-bui-om> 'they are married' (*n=e-bui-om* 'id.') (RB$_2$: 56).

Comparisons:
PGA *n*= '3PL' (Abbi 2013: 174); Akachari <n-> 'they' (Portman 1887: 187)

nimi (NA) *v* (?)
To catch hold (?)

Attestations:
(1) <nimi> 'one who catches hold' (RB$_2$: 118)

Notes:
Recorded as a personal name, it could also be a verb (cf. **kidʒeri**).

nio |n-io| (AKJ, NA) *pron*
They

Attestations:
(1) <nio> [personal pronoun] (RB$_2$: 501) (AKJ)
(2) <nio> 'they' (RB$_2$: 190) (NA)

Comparisons:
PGA *niyo* 'they' (Manoharan 1989: 68)

nu |n-u| (NA) *pron*
They
(1) <n-u-ben-om> 'they sleeping' (*n-u beno-m* 'They are sleeping') (RB$_2$: 501), 'they (are) sleeping' (RB$_2$: 504)

Comparisons:
PGA *nu* '3PL' (Abbi 2013: 69, 257, 287); Akachari <nó> 'they' (Portman 1887: 135, 141, 145, 149, 187)

ŋ= (NA) *pron*
You (sg.)

Attestations:
(1) <ŋ'> 'thou' (RB$_2$: 55), <ŋ-> 'thou' (RB$_2$: 501), <tio ŋ'arai-čulutu-bom> 'I will follow you' (*tio ŋ=arai-ʧulutu-bom* 'id.') (RB$_2$: 55)

Comparisons:
PGA *ŋ*= '2SG' (Abbi 2013: 174); Akachari <ng-> 'you' (Portman 1887: 167, 185)

ŋil= (NA) *pron*
You (pl.)

Attestations:

(1) <ŋil-> 'you' (RB_2: 501)

Comparisons:

PGA *ŋil-* ~ *ŋel-* ~ *ŋol-* ~ *ŋole-* ~ *ŋale-* (Avtans 1996: 56)

ŋilio |ŋil-io| (AKJ, NA) *pron*

You (pl.)

Attestations:

(1) <ŋilio> [personal pronoun] (RB_2: 501) (AKJ)
(2) <ŋilio t-ače-bom> 'you (pl.) come with (accompany) me' (*ŋilio t=a-tʃe-bom* 'you (pl.) are accompanying me') (RB_2: 501) (NA)

Comparisons:

PGA *ŋilie* ~ *ŋilio* 'you (pl.)' (Abbi 2012: 307, 374)

ŋio |ŋ-io| (AKJ, NA) *pron*

You (sg.)

Attestations:

(1) <ŋio> [personal pronoun] (RB_2: 501) (AKJ)
(2) <ŋio t-ače-bom> 'you are coming with me' (*ŋio t=a-tʃe-bom* 'you (sg.) are accompanying me') (RB_2: 504) (NA)

Comparisons:

PGA *ŋio* 'you (sg.)' (Abbi 2012: 306, 371); Akachari <ngíó> 'thou' (Portman 1887: 83), 'you' (Portman 1887: 91)

ɲuri (NA) *n*

Fish sp.: *Plotosus* sp.

Attestations:

(1) <nyuri> '*Plotosus* sp.' (RB_2: 221), <ńyuri> 'a fish that is found in the creeks' (RB_2: 96–7)

Comparisons:

PGA *ɲure* 'eel; fish' (Abbi 2012: 375); Akabo <ńyuri> 'fish found in inland creeks' (RB_2: 97), '*Plotosus* sp. probably *P. arab*' (RB_2: 103)

odu (AKJ, NA) *n*

K.o. clay

Attestations:

(1) <odu> 'a kind of light coloured clay' (RB_1: 39), 'clay' (RB_2: 106) (AKJ)

(2) <odu> 'clay' (RB_2: 90, 97, 99, 111, 114, 122, 281, 312, 484), 'common clay' (RB_2: 121, 122), 'commoner clay' (RB_2: 180), [clay] (RB_2: 313) (NA)

Comparisons:

PGA *oḍu* 'clay' (Abbi 2012: 375); Akachari <ótó> 'white clay' (Portman 1887: 213)

Notes:

Cf. **akaodu** and **tɔlodu**.

oitʃolo (NA) *v*

To have in adoption

Attestations:

(1) <t'oi-čolo-kom> 'adopted child, he whom I have adopted' (*t=oitʃolo-kom* '(who) I have in adoption') (RB_2: 68)

okoʤumu |oko-ʤumu| (AKJ, NA) *n*

Medicine-man

Attestations:

(1) <oko-ǰumu> 'medicine-man, one who speaks from dreams' (RB_2: 48) (AKJ)

(2) <oko-ǰumu> 'medicine-man' (RB_2: 51, 157, 164, 176, 301), [medicine-man] (RB_2: 177–9, 306) 'dreamer' (RB_2: 167, 301) (NA)

Comparisons:

PGA *okoɟumu* 'man who is possessed by evil; spirit medium' (Abbi 2012: 375)

Notes:

Cf. **otʤumu**.

okotaliŋ kolɔt |oko-taliŋ kolɔt| (NA) *n*

A boy after his back was scarified in an initiation ceremony and before the turtle-eating ceremony (**tʃokbiʤo** or **tʃokbi kimil**)

Attestations:

(1) <oko-taliŋ-kolo̲t> 'boy [after scarification]' (RB_2: 95)

Notes:

'The boy does not receive a new name on this occasion [the scarification – RZ/BC], but for a few weeks his own name is dropped and he is addressed and spoken as *Eǰido*. From this time the boy is

described as being *oko-taliŋ-kolo̲t*, this being the masculine term corresponding to *aka-ndu-kolo̲t* for girls' (RB$_2$: 95).
The meaning of **kolɔt** is uncertain, perhaps 'boy, girl'.

okɔr (AKJ) *n*
Plant sp.

Attestations:
(1) <oko̲r> [flower-name] (RB$_2$: 119)

olo (AKJ) *n*
Adze

Attestations:
(1) <olo> 'an adze' (RB$_1$: 39)

Comparisons:
Akachari <ólo> 'adze'

omrap |om-rap| (AKJ) *n*
Spine

Attestations:
(1) <òm-rap> 'spine' (M: 172)

Comparisons:
PGA *onrɛːpt̪ɔːy* 'backbone' (Abbi 2012: 376); Akachari <mam réb> [*sic*] 'spine' (*m-om-rep* 'our spine') (Portman 1887: 75)

oŋba |oŋ-ba| (AKJ) *n*
Fleshy portion of the forearm

Attestations:
(1) <ông-bâ> 'fore-arm (fleshy portion)' (M: 169)

Notes:
The nasal segment could be *m*.

oŋbrɔno |oŋ-brɔno| (AKJ) *n*
Ankle

Attestations:
(1) <òng-bròno> 'ankle' (M: 169)

Comparisons:
PGA *oŋrɔno* 'ankle' (Abbi 2012: 376), *t̪ʰumrɔnɔ* 'my ankle' (Kumar 2001: 107)

Notes:
This is the only example we have of a syllable-initial consonant cluster, and the *b* may be epenthetic; it is absent from the corresponding PGA forms, but cf., however, *omrap* 'spine' with the same somatic prefix *oŋ-* ~ *om-* (3.2.1.5) and no *b*.

oŋkara |oŋ-kara| (AKJ) *n*
Nail (of finger or toe)

Attestations:
(1) <òng-kâra> 'nail (of finger or toe)' (M: 171)

Comparisons:
PGA *oŋkara* 'nail' (Abbi 2012: 376)

oŋkide |oŋ-kide| (AKJ) *n*
Knuckle

Attestations:
(1) <òng-kide> 'knuckle' (M: 171)

oŋkɔra |oŋ-kɔra| (AKJ, NA) *n*

1. Hand

Attestations:
(1) <òng-kōra> 'hand' (M: 170) (AKJ)
(2) <oŋ-ko̱ra> 'hand' (RB_2: 24) (NA)

2. Finger

Attestations:
(1) <òng-kōra> 'finger' (M: 170) (AKJ)

Comparisons:
PGA *kʰoːra* 'hand' (Abbi 2012: 365), *ɔŋkara* 'finger' (Abbi 2012: 378); Akachari <móng kora tumeku> 'palm of the hand' (*m-oŋ-kɔra tumeku* 'our palm of the hand') (Portman 1887: 55)

oŋkɔro |oŋ-kɔro| (NA) *n*
Hand

Attestations:
(1) <ŋ-oŋ-ko̱ro ko> 'in thy hand' (RB_2: 503)

Comparisons:
PGA *ɔŋkorɔ* 'hand' (Abbi 2012: 378)

Notes:
Apparently, a variant form of **oŋkɔra**.

oŋkɔtra |oŋ-kɔtra| (AKJ) *n*

1. Palm of the hand

Attestations:
(1) <òng-kōtra> 'palm' (M: 171)

2. Sole of the foot

Attestations:
(1) <òng-kōtra> 'sole of the foot' (M: 171)

oŋkuʤu |oŋ-kuʤu| (AKJ) *n*
Knuckle

Attestations:
(1) <òng-kûǰu> 'knuckle' (M: 171)

oŋmatɔ |oŋ-matɔ| (AKJ) *n*
Foot

Attestations:
(1) <òng-mâ-tō> 'foot' (M: 170)

Comparisons:
PGA *oma:ṭṭɔ* 'foot' (Abbi 2012: 375); Akachari <óma tāū> 'id.'

Notes:
The first nasal segment could be *m*.

oŋpoŋ |oŋ-poŋ| (AKJ) *n*
Armpit

Attestations:
(1) <ông-pông> 'arm-pit' (M: 169)

Comparisons:
PGA *omp*^{h}*oŋ* ~ *oŋp*^{h}*oŋ* 'armpit' (Abbi 2012: 376); Akachari <óm póng> 'id.' (Portman 1887: 165)

Notes:
The first nasal segment could be *m*. Cf. **akapoŋ** and **ɛrapoŋ**.

oŋtɔi |oŋ-tɔi| (AKJ) *n*
Wrist

Attestations:

(1) <òng-tō> [*sic*] 'wrist' (M: 172)

Comparisons:

PGA *oŋʈɔe* 'wrist bone' (Abbi 2012: 376)

otareptʃip |ot-are(u)p(u)-tʃip| (NA) *n*

Older woman of the same generation

Attestations:

(1) <ot-arep-čip> 'any person of the speaker's generation who is older than himself (…) fem.' (RB_2: 55)

Notes:

Synonym: **ototoatuetʃip**.

otareupu |ot-areupu| (NA) *n*

Older person of the same generation

Attestations:

(1) <ot-areupu> 'any person of the speaker's generation who is older than himself' (RB_2: 55)

Notes:

'An alternative word of exactly the same meaning [as **ototoatue** – RZ/BC] is *ot-areupu* (fem. *ot-arep-čip*)' (RB_2: 55)

otbetʃ |ot-betʃ| (NA) *n*

Hair

Attestations:

(1) <ra t'ot-betč> 'pig's hair' (*ra t=Ø-ot-ber* 'hair of the pig') (RB_2: 119)

Comparisons:

Cf. PGA *otbec* ~ *otbɛc* 'hair, body hair' (Abbi 2012: 376); Akachari <ót baich> 'hair' (Portman 1887: 167)

Notes:

Cf. **betʃ** and **ɛrbetʃ**.

otbo |ot-bo| (AKJ, NA) *n*

Back

Attestations:

(1) <ôt-bâ> 'back' (M: 169) (AKJ)

(2) <ot-bo> 'the back (of anything)' (RB_2: 24) (NA)

otʤete |ot-ʤete| (AKJ) *adj*

Shy, ashamed

Attestations:

(1) <ot-ǰete> 'shy, ashamed' (RB_2: 81)

Comparisons:

PGA *uɟɟete* 'shy' (Abbi 2012: 395); Akachari <tot jété> 'ashamed' (*t=ot-ʤete* 'I am ashamed') (Portman 1887: 13)

otʤulu$_1$ |ot-ʤulu| (NA) *adj*

Cold

Attestations:

(1) <ot-ǰulu> 'cold' (RB_2: 137, 138)

Comparisons:

PGA *ɟulu* 'cold' (Abbi 2012: 362); Akachari <tót julu> 'cold' (*t=ot-ʤulu* 'I am cold') (Portman 1887: 23)

otʤulu$_2$ |ot-ʤulu| (NA) *n*

Clothes

Attestations:

(1) <Lau ot-ǰulu> 'clothes [of the visitors]' (*lau Ø-ot-ʤulu* 'clothes of a light-skinned person') (RB_2: 138)

Comparisons:

PGA *ɟulu* 'clothes, dress' (Abbi 2012: 362)

otʤumu$_1$ |ot-ʤumu| (NA) *n*

Dream

Attestations:

(1) <ot-ǰumu> 'dream' (RB_2: 166)

Comparisons:

PGA *ɟumu* 'dream' (Abbi 2012: 362); Akachari <áka yumu> 'dream' (Portman 1887: 27)

Notes:

Cf. **okoʤumu**.

otʤumu$_2$ |ot-ʤumu| (NA) *v*

To dream

Attestations:
(1) <ot-ǰumu> 'to dream' (RB$_2$: 166)

otʤumulo |ot-ʤumulo| (NA) *n*

1. Shadow

Attestations:
(1) <ot-ǰumulo> 'shadow' (RB$_2$: 166)

2. Reflection

Attestations:
(1) <ot-ǰumulo> 'reflection' (RB$_2$: 166)

3. Double of the sleeper

Attestations:
(1) <ot-ǰumulo> 'sleeper's double, double of the sleeper' (RB$_2$: 167), 'double' (RB$_2$: 169), 'double, shadow-self, soul' (RB$_2$: 304)

4. Photograph

Attestations:
(1) <ot-ǰumulo> 'photograph' (RB$_2$: 166)

Notes:
'Dreams are sometimes explained by saying that the sleeper's double (*ot-ǰumulo*) has left his body and is wandering elsewhere' (RB$_2$: 167). 'When a man dies his *ot-ǰumulo* (double) goes up to the sky and becomes a Lau (spirit)' (RB$_2$: 169).

otkimil$_1$ |ot-kimil| (NA) *adj*

1. Hot

Attestations:
(1) <ot-kimil> 'hot' (RB$_2$: 266), <ino ot-kimil bi> 'The water is hot' (*ino ot-kimil=bi* 'There is hot water') (RB$_2$: 267)

2. In the condition of having eaten certain foods

Attestations:
(1) <ot-kimil> [one who has eaten food] (RB$_2$: 268–9, 307)

3. Having joined in a dance

Attestations:
(1) <ot-kimil> [one who has joined in a dance] (RB$_2$: 308, 321)

Comparisons:
PGA k^h*imil* 'warm, hot' (Abbi 2012: 364); Akachari <kímil> 'hot' (Portman 1887: 39)

Notes:
'It is probable, then, that when a native says that after eating food he is *ot-kimil* and therefore paints himself with clay he does not mean simply that he is hot' (RB_2: 268).
'(...) the word *ot-kimil*, when it is used to describe the condition of a person who has eaten food, denotes simply this condition of danger, and nothing more' (RB_2: 269).
'When the word is used in reference to a person who has just partaken of food it denotes a condition of danger produced by contact with the power in foods' (RB_2: 307).
'Finally, a man who has joined in a dance is said to be *ot-kimil* and seems to be regarded as being in a condition of danger similar to that produced by food. It might be thought that in this instance the word is only used in its literal meaning of "hot," but I believe that this is not so. The dance is the occasion on which the individual comes most closely into contact with the power in the society itself, and I believe that this contact is regarded as dangerous and therefore as making the individual *ot-kimil*. Thus we see that in its various uses the word *ot-kimil* denotes a condition of danger due to contact with that power on the interaction of the different manifestations of which the well-being of the society depends' (RB_2: 308).
'(...) the dance is a condition of danger by reason of the contact it involves between the individual and the power of the society' (RB_2: 321).

Notes:
Cf. **akakimil**, **ɛrkimil**, **kimil** and **kimil ʤo**.

otkimil$_2$ |ot-kimil| (NA) *v*
To be hot

Attestations:
(1) <t'ot-kimil-bom> 'I am hot' (*t=ot-kimil-bom* 'id.') (RB_2: 267)

otlam |ot-lam| (NA) *adj*
Strong

Attestations:

(1) <ot-lam> 'strong' (RB_2: 498), <e-tomo-t-ot-lam> 'muscularly powerful' (*Ø-e-tomo t=ot-lam* 'His/her flesh is strong') (RB_2: 498), 'muscle strong' (RB_2: 501)

Comparisons:

PGA *erlam* 'strong' (M: 115); Akachari <ódlam> [*sic*] 'strong' (Portman 1887: 79)

otloŋo |ot-loŋo| (AKJ) *n*

Neck

Attestations:

(1) <ōt-lôngo> 'neck' (M: 171)

Comparisons:

Akachari <ot longó> 'neck' (Portman 1887: 53)

otone |ot-one| (NA) *n*

Son-in-law, daughter-in-law

Attestations:

(1) <ot-otone> 'his son-in-law' (*Ø-ot-ot-one* 'id.') (RB_2: 54), 'daughter's husband, son's wife' (RB_2: 56)

Comparisons:

Cf. PGA *otoni* 'daughter's husband, younger sister's husband' (Abbi 2012: 396)

Notes:

ototone seems to be the possessed form of this kin term (see section 3.2.1.6).

ototoatue |ot-otoatue| (NA) *n*

Older person of the same generation

Attestations:

(1) <ot-otoatue> 'he who was born before me' (*Ø-ot-otoatue* 'his older brother' (RB_2: 54, 76), 'his/her older person of the same generation') (RB_2: 55), 'his [older brother]' (RB_2: 76), <t'ot-otoatue ot-tire> 'my older brother's child' (RB_2: 56) (*t-ot-otoatue Ø-ot-tire* 'id.') (NA)

(2) <ot-otoatue> 'he who was born before me' (RB_2: 66–7) (AKJ)

Comparisons:

PGA *ɔttɔwotʰu:we* 'brother' (Abbi 2012: 378)

Notes:

This term does 'not, strictly speaking, convey any idea of consanguinity, although [it is] commonly used to refer to a brother or a sister' (RB$_2$: 67). Synonym: **otarepu**.

ototoatue ottire |ot-otoatue Ø-ot-tire| (lit. 'child of an older person of the same generation') (NA)

Nephew, niece (child of an older brother or sister)

Attestations:

(1) <t'ot-otoatue ot-tire> 'my older brother's child' (*t-ot-otoatue Ø-ot-tire* 'id.') (RB$_2$: 56)

ototoatueʧip |ot-otoatue-ʧip| (NA) *n*

Older woman of the same generation

Attestations:

(1) <ot-otoatue-čip> 'his older sister' (*Ø-ot-otoatue-ʧip* 'id.') (RB$_2$: 54, 56)

Notes:

Synonym: **otareputʃip**.

ottau |ot-tau| (NA) *v*

To be cold

Attestations:

(1) <t-ot-tau-bom> 'I am cold' (*t=ot-tau-bom* 'id.') (RB$_2$: 504)

Comparisons:

PGA *t̪ʰɔo* 'cold' (Abbi 2012: 393)

Notes:

Cf. **tau.** See also section 3.1.

ottei |ot-tei| (AKJ) *n*

Headache

Attestations:

(1) <ot-tei> 'headache' (RB$_2$: 499)

Comparisons:

PGA *ottei* 'headache' (Abbi 2012: 377)

Notes:

Cf. **etei**, **ɛratei** and **tei**.

ottire |ot-tire| (NA) *n*

Child (possessed form)

Attestations:

(1) <ot-tire> 'his child' (*Ø-ot-tire* 'id.') (RB$_2$: 54, 499), 'his or her child' (RB$_2$: 55, 68), 'child of a particular person' (RB$_2$: 499), <t'ot-tire> 'my child' (*t-ot-tire* 'id.') (RB$_2$: 55), <Bora ot-tire> 'the child of Bora' (*bora Ø-ot-tire* 'id.') (RB$_2$: 55), <Biliku ot-tire> 'the "child" of Biliku' (*biliku Ø-ot-tire* 'id.' (RB$_2$: 154)

Comparisons:

PGA *utt*^{h}*ire* 'child' (Abbi 2013: 74, 113, 115, 134, 143, 192, 248, 258, 267, 287); Akachari <ó tíré> 'id.' (Portman 1887: 163)

Notes:

Possessed counterpart of **etire**. 'In the form *ot-tire* the word means "his or her child" with reference to some person understood' (RB$_2$: 68).

otʧo |ot-ʧo| (AKJ, NA) *n*

1. Head

Attestations:

(1) <ot-čo> 'head' (RB$_2$: 498), 'head of something; his, her or its head' (*Ø-ot-ʧo* 'his/her head') (RB$_2$: 501), <t-ot-čo> 'my head' (*t-ot-ʧo* 'id.') (RB$_2$: 501) (AKJ)

(2) <ŋ-ot-čo> 'thy head' (*ŋ-ot-ʧo* 'id.') (RB$_2$: 504), <ra t'ot-čo> 'a pig's head' (*ra t=Ø-ot-ʧo* 'the pig's head') (Radcliffe-Brown 1922: 496; not in RB$_2$) (NA)

2. Fruit

Attestations:

(1) <ot-čo> 'fruit' (RB$_2$: 499)

Comparisons:

PGA *ɛrco* 'head; fruit' (Abbi 2012: 354); Akachari <échu> 'head' (Portman 1887: 37), <ér chu> 'fruit' (Portman 1887: 35)

1. Prow (see **roa**)

Notes:

Cf. **ɛrʧo**.

ɔrʧubi (AKJ, NA)

Snake sp.: *Ophiophagus elaps*

Attestations:

(1) <o̱r-čubi> 'a species of snake' (RB$_2$: 124) (AKJ)

(2) <or-čubi> 'a species of large snake' (RB$_2$: 317, 484), 'snake' (RB$_2$: 373) (NA)

Comparisons:

PGA *ɔrʃubi* ~ *orʃubi* 'snake' (Abbi 2012: 376, 242); Akabo <or-čubi> 'snake' (RB$_2$: 97); Akachari <ór chubí> 'snake (*Ophiophagus elaps*)' (Portman 1887: 73)

Notes:

Cf. **ʧubi**.

ɔrʧubi tɛrabat |ɔrʧubi t=Ø-ɛra-bat| (lit. 'tail of the *Ophiophagus elaps* snake') (AKJ, NA)

Design of zig-zag lines painted on the body with white clay

Attestations:

(1) <o̲r-čubi t'e̲ra-bat> 'one customary pattern' (RB$_2$: 124) (AKJ)

(2) <or-čubi t'era-bat> 'design of zig-zag lines painted on the body with white clay' (RB$_2$: 484) (NA)

pare (AKJ) *n*

Plant sp.

Attestations:

(1) <pare> 'a plant' (RB$_2$: 183)

pata (NA) *n*

Mushroom sp. (?)

Attestations:

(1) <pata> [a vegetable food] (RB$_2$: 199)

Comparisons:

PGA *pata* 'mushroom' (Abbi 2012: 379)

peʧ (AKJ, NA) *n*

Pot

Attestations:

(1) <peč> 'a cooking pot' (RB$_1$: 39, 48), 'pot' (RB$_1$: 40; RB$_2$: 474) (AKJ)

(2) <peč> 'pot' (RB$_2$: 497) (NA)

Comparisons:

PGA *p*^{h}*ɛc* 'pot' (Abbi 2012: 379); Akachari <paich> 'id.' (Portman 1887: 157), <péit> 'cooking-pot' (Portman 1887: 208)

Notes:

'One of the very few words which is the same in all Andamanese languages is the word for pot, *buču* in the Little Andaman, *buǰ* in Aka-Bea and *peč* in Aka-Jeru' (RB$_2$: 474). This word is particularly close in form and meaning to Proto-Austroasiatic *buəc 'k.o. small vessel' (Shorto 2006: 246) with reflexes in Monic (Mon *pòt* 'small pot or cup') and Khmer (*pù:əc* '(small) jar'). Archaeological excavations on Great Andaman revealed that pottery was introduced in the Andamans at a fairly early stage (see the occurrence of potsherds in the basal layers of the Chauldari midden (South Andaman), for which a radiocarbon date on marine shells of 2280±90 BP has been obtained) and that, in terms of quality of manufacture, it appears to degenerate with time (Cooper 2002: 87). The strong affinity of the Great Andamanese terms for 'pot' to the reconstructed Proto-Austroasiatic denoting a type of vessel might indicate that pottery arrived in Great Andaman from contact with an old (visiting) Austroasiatic-speaking people. The Önge (Little Andaman) and Jarawa terms for 'pot' (*bu:tʃʰu* in Jarawa; Kumar 2012: 62) also resemble Proto-Austroasiatic **buəc*, but even more so Akabea and Akarbale *budʒ*. This suggests that the terms in question were borrowed from Akabea or, perhaps, Proto-South Andamanese (the common parent language of Akabea and Akarbale).

piletʃar (AKJ) *n*

High-tide

Attestations:

(1) <pilečar> 'high-tide' (RB_2: 101)

Comparisons:

Cf. PGA *epʰile* 'tide' (Abbi 2012: 347) and *sarepʰile* 'tide, high tide, tsunami' (Abbi 2012: 383)

Notes:

Cf. **tʃari**.

piɲ (AKJ (?)) *n*

Tree sp.

Attestations:

(1) <piń́> [a tree] (RB_2: 201)

pir (AKJ) *n*

1. Palm sp.: *Calamus* sp.

Attestations:

(1) <pir> 'a kind of cane (Calamus)' (RB_1: 39), 'particular species of large cane, cane' (RB_2: 146)

2. Rainbow

Attestations:

(1) <pir> 'rainbow' (RB$_2$: 146)

Comparisons:

PGA $p^{h}ir$ 'cane' (Abbi 2012: 379); Akachari <pír> 'common cane' (Portman 1887: 226), 'rainbow' (Portman 1887: 63)

Notes:

'The Andamanese have certain legends regarding the use of the rainbow, and these have been hitherto understood as referring to 'canes." (RB$_2$: 146).

piribi (AKJ) *n*

Storm (?)

Attestations:

(1) <piribi> 'storm' (RB$_2$: 193)

Comparisons:

Akachari <piribi> 'storm' (RB$_2$: 202)

Notes:

'I have the word *piribi* in my notes as meaning a storm, but the translation is doubtful' (RB$_2$: 202).

poramo (NA) *n*

Tree sp.: *Myristica longifolia*

Attestations:

(1) <poramo> 'Myristica longifolia' (RB$_2$: 92)

poruatɔko (AKJ, NA) *n*

Bird sp.

Attestations:

(1) <poruatoko> [a bird] (RB$_2$: 199) (AKJ)

(2) <poruato̲ko> [a bird] (RB$_2$: 199) (NA)

pɔitʃo (AKJ, NA) *n*

Tree sp.: *Sterculia macrophylla*

Attestations:

(1) <po̲ičo> 'Sterculia tree' (RB$_1$: 39), '*Sterculia*' (RB$_2$: 192) (AKJ)

(2) <po̲ičo tomo> 'wood (literally flesh) of the *Sterculia* (*po̲ičo*) tree' (*pɔitʃo tomo* 'id.') (RB$_2$: 119) (NA)

Comparisons:
PGA p^h*oco* 'tree' (Abbi 2012: 379), *pocho 'Sterculia macrophylla'* (Awasthi 1991: 278); Akachari <póchó> 'Sterculia (villosa?)' (Portman 1887: 217)

pɔrɔto (AKJ) *n*
Palm sp.: *Caryota mitis*

Attestations:
(1) <po̲ro̲to> 'Caryota palm' (RB$_1$: 39; RB$_2$: 497)

Comparisons:
PGA p^h*ɔrɔto* 'tree; fruit' (Abbi 2012: 380), *phoroto 'Caryota mitis* Lour.' (Awasthi 1991: 279); Akachari <pāūratāū> 'Caryota sobolifera' (Portman 1887: 217)

pɔrubi (NA) *n*
Frog sp.

Attestations:
(1) <Maia Po̲rubi> 'Sir Frog' (RB$_2$: 221–2), <Po̲rubi> [Frog] (RB$_2$: 221–2)

Comparisons:
PGA p^h*orube* 'frog' (Abbi 2012: 380); Akachari <pórubé> 'id.' (Portman 1887: 35)

pu (NA) *part*
NEGATIVE

Attestations:
(1) <-pu> 'negative suffix' (RB$_2$: 503)

Comparisons:
PGA p^h*o* ~ p^h*u* 'negative marker' (Abbi 2013: 254); Akachari <pu> [id.] (Portman 1887: 103, 105, 107, 121, 129, 145, 149, 155)

pulimu (NA) *n*
Fly sp.

Attestations:
(1) <pulimu> 'fly' (RB$_2$: 221), <Maia Pulimu> 'Sir Fly' (RB$_2$: 220)

Comparisons:
PGA p^h*ulɛmu* 'fly' (Abbi 2012: 380); Akachari <pulímu> 'fly' (Portman 1887: 33)

puliu (AKJ) *n*

Tree sp.: *Terminalia procera*

Attestations:

(1) <puliu> [flower-name] (RB$_2$: 119)

Comparisons:

Akachari <póeló> 'Terminalia procera' (Portman 1887: 217) (cf. Akakede <pólíe> 'id.'; Portman 1887: 217)

ra (AKJ, NA) *n*

Pig

Attestations:

(1) <ra> 'pig' (RB$_1$: 39; RB$_2$: 498) (AKJ)

(2) <ra t'ot-betč> 'pig's hair' (*ra t=Ø-ot-betʃ* 'hair of the pig') (RB$_2$: 119), <ra t'e̱ra-puli> 'pig pattern' (*ra t=Ø-ɛra-puli* 'pattern of the pig') (RB$_2$: 123), <ra-taru> 'boar (male pig)' (*ra taru* 'id.') (RB$_2$: 504), <ra t'er-kuro> 'a big pig' (*ra t=ɛr-kuro* 'the big pig') (Radcliffe-Brown 1922: 496; not in RB$_2$), <ra t'ot-čo> 'a pig's head' (*ra t=Ø-ot-tʃo* 'the pig's head') (Radcliffe-Brown 1922: 496; not in RB$_2$) (NA)

Comparisons:

PGA *ra* 'pig' (Abbi 2012: 381); Akachari <rá> 'id.' (Portman 1887: 57)

Notes:

All other languages of the Great Andamanese family have similar forms for 'pig': Akabea *reg*, Akarbale *rak*, Opuchikwar and Okojuwoi *re*, Okol *reak*, Akakede *ra*. These forms are also more or less similar to their equivalents in Old Mon and Old Khmer, respectively *clik* and *ɟroːk* or *ɟrɔːk* 'id.' (mod. *cruːk*) (Jenner 2009: 166) (cf. Proto-Austroasiatic *lik[ ]/*liik[ ] 'id.' (Shorto 2006: 160); the square brackets of the proto-form indicate that it could contain something else not yet specifiable). Although the available archaeological evidence does not satisfactorily resolve the question regarding the presence of the wild pig (*Sus scrofa*) on the Andaman Islands (Cooper 2002: 158), it is interesting to note that an Opuchikwar legend gathered by Radcliffe-Brown (1922: 217) seems to indicate that pigs were introduced into Great Andaman as domesticates and later became feral (Heine-Geldern 1963). The possibility that the pig was imported to Great Andaman from an old (visiting) Austroasiatic-speaking people, for the moment, cannot therefore be excluded.

re (AKJ) *n*

Plant sp.

Attestations:

(1) <re> [flower-name] (AKJ) (RB_2: 191)

remu (NA) *n*

Iron

Attestations:

(1) <remu t̠oi> 'piece of iron' (*remu tɔi* 'bone of the iron') (RB_2: 118)

Comparisons:

PGA *remo* 'iron'

remu tɔi (lit. 'bone of the iron') (NA)

Piece of iron

Attestations:

(1) <remu t̠oi> 'piece of iron' (RB_2: 118)

reŋko (NA) *n*

Green pigeon

Attestations:

(1) <reŋko> 'green pigeon' (RB_2: 91) (NA)

Comparisons:

PGA *rɛnkɔ* 'Andaman green pigeon, *Treron chloropterus*' (Pande and Abbi 2011: 36), 'pigeon' (Abbi 2012: 382)

reŋo (AKJ, NA) *n*

Tree sp.: *Ficus laccifera*

Attestations:

(1) <reŋo> 'Ficus tree' (RB_1: 39), 'Ficus' (RB_2: 497) (AKJ)
(2) <reŋko> [*sic*] '*Ficus laccifera*' (RB_2: 91, 157) (NA)

Comparisons:

PGA *reŋo* 'Ficus tree' (Abbi 2012: 381), *rengo* 'Ficus sp.; *Ficus retusa* L. var. *nitida* Thunb.' (Awasthi 1991: 278)

Notes:

Radcliffe-Brown indicates that '[t]he same name, *Reŋko*, is used to denote both the green pigeon and also the *Ficus laccifera*, of the fruit of which the pigeon is very fond' (RB_2: 91). In fact, the green pigeon and the *Ficus laccifera* have different names in North Andamanese (the former is **reŋko**), although they may well be etymological doublets.

reɲa (NA) *n*

Possessions

Attestations:

(1) <renya čope> 'much baggage, many possessions' (*reɲa ʧope* 'many possessions') (RB$_2$: 119)

Comparisons:

PGA *reɲa* 'things' (Abbi 2012: 381); Akachari <árá rinya> 'package' (Portman 1887: 54)

reo (NA) *n*

Insect sp.

Attestations:

(1) <reo> 'a species of insect making a noise like a cicada' (RB$_2$: 156)

roa (AKJ, NA) *n*

Canoe

Attestations:

(1) <roa> 'canoe' (RB$_2$: 499) (AKJ)

(2) <t-ičo roa> 'my canoe' (*t-iʧo roa* 'id.') (RB$_2$: 504), <Buio ičo roa> 'Buio's canoe' (*buyo Ø-iʧo roa* 'id.'), <t-ičo roa t-er-kuro> 'my canoe is big' (*t-iʧo roa t=ɛr-kuro*) (RB$_2$: 504) (NA)

Comparisons:

PGA *roːɔ* 'canoe, dongi' (Abbi 2012: 382); Akachari <róá ~ róāū> 'canoe' (Portman 1887: 19, 121, 147)

Notes:

An Austroasiatic origin of this word is probable, as suggested by its Akabea and Akarbale equivalent *roko*, which appears rather close phonetically to the Proto-Austroasiatic form *ɗu(u)k 'boat, canoe' reconstructed by Shorto (2006: 144). In the remaining Great Andamanese languages 'canoe' is *ro* (Opuchikwar, Okojuwoi, Akakede) or *rɔ* (Okol).

roa totʧo |roa t=Ø-ot-ʧo| (lit. 'head of the canoe') (AKJ)

Prow of a canoe

Attestations:

(1) <roa-t-ot-čo> 'prow of a canoe' (RB$_2$: 499) (AKJ)

Comparisons:

PGA *rowatɛrco* 'front of the dongi (k.o. boat)' (Abbi 2012: 113)

roputʃ (AKJ, NA) *n*

One who has lost a brother or sister

Attestations:

(1) <ropuč> 'one who has lost a brother or sister' (RB$_2$: 112) (AKJ)
(2) <ropuč> 'one who has lost a brother or sister' (RB$_2$: 121) (NA)

Comparisons:

PGA *rɔpuc* 'one who loses a sibling' (Abbi 2012: 382)

t= (AKJ, NA) *art*

DEFINITE ARTICLE

Attestations:

(1) <o̲r-čubi t'e̲ra-bat> 'one customary pattern' (*ɔrtʃubi t=Ø-ɛra-bat* 'tail of the *Ophiophagus elaps* snake') (RB$_2$: 124), <roa-t-ot-čo> 'prow of a canoe' (*roa t=Ø-ot-tʃo* 'head of the canoe') (RB$_2$: 499), <ti-t-e̲ra-lobuŋ> 'a long way' (*ti t=ɛra-lobuŋ* 'the long place') (RB$_2$: 500) (AKJ)
(2) <t-> integrative particle, integrative prefix (RB$_2$: 503), <ra t'ot-betč> 'pig's hair' (*ra t=Ø-ot-betʃ* 'hair of the pig') (RB$_2$: 119), <čokbi t'e̲ra-puli> 'turtle pattern' (*tʃokbi t=Ø-ɛra-puli* 'pattern of the turtle') (RB$_2$: 123), <ra t'e̲ra-puli> 'pig pattern' (*ra t=Ø-ɛra-puli* 'pattern of the pig') (RB$_2$: 123), <toto t'e̲ra-puli> 'pattern (...) used (...) to decorate a girl after the ceremony at her first menstruation' (*toto t=Ø-ɛra-puli* 'pattern of the pandanus') (RB$_2$: 124), <lau t'e̲r-čo> 'skull [of a dead person]' (*lau t=Ø-ɛr-tʃo* 'skull of the dead person') (RB$_2$: 137), <Lau t'ara-nyu> 'Penal Settlement [of Port Blair], the village of the spirits' (*lau t=Ø-ara-ɲu* 'village of the spirits') (RB$_2$: 137), <Lau t'e̲r-kuro> 'mythical ancestor' (*lau t=ɛr-kuro* 'the big spirit') (RB$_2$: 137), <Lau t'er-kuro> 'ancestor' (RB$_2$: 190), <kimil-t'e̲ra-puli> 'a pattern' (*kimil t=Ø-ɛra-puli* 'pattern of the boy or girl during the turtle-eating ceremony') (RB$_2$: 314), <or-čubi t'era-bat> 'design of zig-zag lines painted on the body with white clay' (*ɔrtʃubi t=Ø-ɛra-bat* 'tail of the *Ophiophagus elaps* snake') (RB$_2$: 484), <e-tomo-t-ot-lam> 'muscularly powerful' (*Ø-e-tomo t=ot-lam* 'his/her flesh is strong') (RB$_2$: 498), 'muscle strong' (RB$_2$: 501), <ko̲roin t-er-kuro> 'a big dugong' (*kɔroin t=ɛr-kuro* 'the big dugong') (RB$_2$: 504), <t-ičo roa t-er-kuro> 'my canoe is big' (*t-itʃo roa t=ɛr-kuro* 'id.') (RB$_2$: 504), <ra t'er-kuro> 'a big pig' (*ra t=ɛr-kuro* 'the big pig') (Radcliffe-Brown 1922: 496; not in RB$_2$), <ra t'ot-čo> 'a pig's head' (*ra t=Ø-ot-tʃo* 'the pig's head') (Radcliffe-Brown 1922: 496; not in RB$_2$) (NA)

Comparisons:

PGA *t=*; Akachari <t-> (Portman 1887: *passim*)

Notes:

The available descriptions of PGA do not recognise a proclitic definite article *t=*, but contain numerous occurrences of this morpheme (such as *fɛc t=a-p^{h}oŋ* 'mouth of the vessel' and *ɲo t=ara-taŋ* 'roof of the house' in Abbi (2013: 159, 206)), which Abbi (2013: 156–62) analyses as a marker of an inanimate possessor; see section 4.1.3. The definite article *t=* also occurs in the following Akajeru noun phrases before a noun whose meaning is obscure: **toto tɛrbua, toto tɛrmɔi, toto tɛrŋau, toto tɛrɲarab** (see below **toto**).

t= (AKJ, NA) *pron*

I, me

Attestations:

(1) <t'a-Ǐeru> 'I am Aka-Jeru' (*t=a-ʤeru* 'id.') (RB$_2$: 24) (AKJ)

(2) <t-> 'I' (RB$_2$: 501), <t'oi-čolo-kom> 'adopted child, he whom I have adopted' (*t=oiʧolo-kom* '(who) I have in adoption') (RB$_2$: 68), <t'ot-kimil-bom> 'I am hot' (*t=ot-kimil-bom* 'id.') (RB$_2$: 267), <ŋilio t-ače-bom> 'you (pl.) come with (accompany) me' (*ŋilio t=a-ʧe-bom* 'you (pl.) are accompanying me') (RB$_2$: 501), <t-u-boto-ba> 'I fell' (*t=uboto-ba* 'id.') (RB$_2$: 503), <ŋio t-ače-bom> 'you are coming with me' (*ŋio t=a-ʧe-bom* 'you (sg.) are accompanying me') (RB$_2$: 504), <t-ot-tau-bom> 'I am cold' (*t=ot-tau-bom* 'id.') (RB$_2$: 504) (NA)

Comparisons:

PGA *ʈ^h=* '1SG' (Abbi 2013: 174); Akabo <t'a-Bo> 'I am Aka-Bo' (*t=a-bo* 'id.') (RB$_2$: 24); Akachari <t-> 'I' (Portman 1887: 97, 153)

taka (AKJ) *n*

Bird sp.

Attestations:

(1) <taka> [a bird] (RB$_2$: 199)

Comparisons:

PGA *ʈaka* 'Pacific reef heron, *Egretta sacra*' (Pande and Abbi 2011: 5), 'heron' (Abbi 2012: 389)

talar (NA) *n*

K.o. soft red stone

Attestations:

(1) <talar> 'a soft red stone' (RB$_2$: 179)

Comparisons:
PGA *t̪aːlar* 'stone' (Abbi 2012: 389)

tarai (AKJ, NA) *n*
A male supernatural being

Attestations:
(1) <Tarai>; cf. RB$_2$, pp. 192, 199, 201, 206, 348 and 370 (AKJ)
(2) <Tarai> 'a being' (RB$_2$: 145, 147, 163, 178), 'an anthropomorphic being' (RB$_2$: 377), <Maia Tarai> [Sir Tarai] (RB$_2$: 150) (NA)

Notes:
'In the North Andaman *Tarai* is declared to be male and *Biliku* female. It can readily be shown that this results from the position of *Biliku* and *Tarai* as regulating the seasons. *Tarai* rules over the rainy season, in which the chief food is the flesh of animals of the land and of the sea; it is the business of men to provide flesh-food. On the contrary *Biliku* rules over the seasons in which the chief foods are vegetable products of different kinds; it is the business of women to provide such foods' (RB$_2$: 365–6).
'*Biliku* and *Tarai* are personifications of the N.E. and S.W. monsoons; as such they are responsible for the weather; feelings awakened by the weather are therefore referred to *Biliku* and *Tarai*' (RB$_2$: 375).

Comparisons:
PGA *tʰarae* 'deity; monsoon storm; monsoon season' (Abbi 2012: 386); Akabo, Akachari, Akakhora <Tarai> (RB$_2$: 147, 150, 199)

tarai bɔto (lit. 'Tarai wind') (AKJ, NA) *n*
South-west wind

Attestations:
(1) <Tarai boto> 'S. W. Wind' (RB$_2$: 147) (AKJ)
(2) <Tarai bo̲to> 'the Tarai wind' (RB$_2$: 377) (NA)

Notes:
'(…) in the North Andaman *Biliku* and *Tarai* are used as the names of the two chief winds' (RB$_2$: 378).

taraiʧulik |tarai-ʧulik| (AKJ, NA) *adv*
Afterwards

Attestations:
(1) <t-arai-čul-ik> 'afterwards' (RB$_2$: 501) (AKJ)
(2) <tarai-čulik> 'afterwards' (RB$_2$: 55) (NA)

tare (AKJ) *n*

Tree sp.

Attestations:

(1) <tare> 'a small tree' (RB_2: 183)

Comparisons:

Akabo <tare> [a plant] (RB_2: 103)

tarendʒek (NA) *adj* (?)

Angry (or nickname for a violent man)

Attestations:

(1) <tarenǰek> 'angry' (RB_2: 119)

Notes:

This word is said to be used a special nickname for '[a] man who is liable to outbursts of violent anger' (RB_2: 49).

taru (NA) *adj*

Male

Attestations:

(1) <ra-taru> 'boar (male pig)' (*ra taru* 'id.') (RB_2: 504)

Comparisons:

PGA *caoʈʰaro* 'male dog' (Abbi 2012: 337), *teoʈʰaro* 'male crocodile' (Abbi 2012: 387)

Notes:

Cf. **etaru**.

tau (AKJ, NA) *n*

Sky

Attestations:

(1) <tau> 'sky' (RB_2: 193) (AKJ)
(2) <tau> 'sky' (RB_2: 144) (NA)

Comparisons:

PGA *ʈao* ~ *ʈɔo* ~ *ʈɔ:* 'sky' (Abbi 2012: 390, 393); Akachari <tāōo> [*sic*] 'id.' (Portman 1887: 73)

Notes:

Cf. **ottau**.

tau meo (lit. 'sky stone') (NA) *n*

'Lapidary sky'

Attestations:

(1) <tau-meo> 'the sky-stone' (RB$_2$: 145) (NA)

Notes:

In North Andaman, the sky 'is regarded as being made of stone (or rock) and is called *tau-meo* (the sky-stone)' (RB$_2$: 145).

tei (AKJ, NA) *n*

Blood

Attestations:

(1) <tei> 'blood' (RB$_2$: 500), <čokbi-tei> 'turtle-blood' (*tʃokbi tei* 'id.') (RB$_2$: 498) (AKJ)

(2) <tei> 'blood' (RB$_2$: 499), <lau-tei> 'spirit blood' (*lau tei* 'id.') (RB$_2$: 119), <čokbi-tei> 'turtle-blood' (RB$_2$: 296) (NA)

Comparisons:

PGA *etei* 'blood' (Abbi 2012: 351); Akachari <été> 'id.' (Portman 1887: 17)

Notes:

Cf. **etei, ɛratei** and **ottei.**

teo (AKJ) *n*

Bird sp.

Attestations:

(1) <teo> [a bird] (RB$_2$: 199)

terkobito (NA) *n*

Centipede

Attestations:

(1) <terkobito-balo> '"centipede creeper" (*Pothos sandens*)' (RB$_2$: 99)

Comparisons:

PGA *tɛrkobito:* 'centipede' (Abbi 2012: 387)

terkobito balo (lit. 'centipede creeper') (NA) *n*

Creeper sp.: *Pothos sandens*

Attestations:

(1) <terkobito-balo> '"centipede creeper" (*Pothos sandens*)' (RB$_2$: 99)

tetʃ (NA) *n*

Leaf

Attestations:

(1) <bido teč lau> 'spirit of the *Calamus* leaf' (RB$_2$: 136), <bido-teč lau> 'jungle spirit' (RB$_2$: 165), <bido-teč-lau> '*Calamus* leaf spirit' (RB$_2$: 292)

Comparisons:

PGA *tec* 'leaf' (Abbi 2012: 386); Akachari <teč> (RB$_2$: 189), <taich> 'id.' (Portman 1887: 159)

tɛraitʃiro |tɛrai-tʃiro| (AKJ) *adv*

Yesterday

Attestations:

(1) <t-e̱rai-čiro> 'yesterday' (RB$_2$: 500)

ti (AKJ) *n*

Place

Attestations:

(1) <ti-t-e̱ra-lobuŋ> 'a long way' [*sic*] (*ti t=ɛra-lobuŋ* 'the long place') (RB$_2$: 500)

Comparisons:

PGA *t̪*^{h}*i* 'place, earth, land' (Abbi 2012: 391); Akachari <tí> 'place' (Portman 1887: 177)

timiku |ti-miku| (NA) *n*

Forest, jungle

Attestations:

(1) <ti-miku> 'forest, land' (RB$_2$: 136), 'forest' (RB$_2$: 199)

Comparisons:

PGA *t̪*^{h}*imik*^{h}*u* 'forest, place' (Abbi 2012: 391); Akachari <tímíku> 'jungle' (Portman 1887: 105, 115), <tíméku> 'id.' (Portman 1887: 131)

Notes:

Cf. **aramiku**, **ɛrmiku** and **maramiku**.

timiku lau (NA) *n*

Spirit of the forest

Attestations:

(1) <ti-miku lau> 'spirits that haunt the jungles' (RB$_2$: 136)

Notes:

Cf. **lau** and **timiku**.

tio |t-io| (AKJ, NA) *n*

I

Attestations:

(1) <tio> [personal pronoun] (RB$_2$: 501), <tio ŋ-arai-čulutu-bom> 'I follow thee' (*tio ŋ=arai-tʃulutu-bom* 'id.') (RB$_2$: 501) (AKJ)

(2) <tio> 'I' (RB$_2$: 55), <tio ŋ'arai-čulutu-bom> 'I will follow you' (*tio ŋ=arai-tʃulutu-bom* 'id.') (RB$_2$: 55), <tio bi tuŋ-om> 'I want (I am wanting)' (*tio=bi tuŋ-om* 'id.') (RB$_2$: 503) (NA)

Comparisons:

PGA *t̪*^{h}*io* 'I' (Abbi 2013: 306, 391); Akachari <tío> 'id.' (Portman 1887: 39)

tip (AKJ) *n*

Tree sp.

Attestations:

(1) <tip> 'a tree' (RB$_2$: 183)

tiriɲ (AKJ) *n*

Kingfisher sp.

Attestations:

(1) <tiriń> 'a species of kingfisher' (RB$_2$: 202)

Comparisons:

PGA *t*^{h}*iriŋ* 'small blue kingfisher, *Alcedo atthis bengalensis*' (Pande and Abbi 2011: 56), 'kingfisher' (Abbi 2012: 388)

tiritmo (AKJ (?), NA) *n*

Kingfisher sp.

Attestations:

(1) <Maia Tiritmo> 'Sir Kingfisher' (RB$_2$: 201) (AKJ (?))

(2) <Maia Tiritmo> 'Sir Kingfisher' (RB$_2$: 201) (NA)

titʃo |t-itʃo| (AKJ, NA) *pron*

Mine, my

Attestations:

(1) <tičo maia> 'my father' (*t-itʃo maya* 'id.') (RB$_2$: 66) (AKJ)

(2) <t-ičo> 'mine' (RB$_2$: 503), <kidi t-ičo bi> (*kidi t-itʃo=bi*) 'this is mine' (RB$_2$: 503), <t-ičo roa> 'my canoe' (RB$_2$: 504), <t-ičo roa t-er-kuro> 'my canoe is big' (*t-itʃo roa t=ɛr-kuro* 'id.') (RB$_2$: 504) (NA)

Comparisons:

PGA *t̪*^{h}*ico* 'my' (Abbi 2012: 391); Akachari <téchuāū> [*sic*] 'id.' (Portman 1887: 115)

Notes:

The noun phrase <tičo maia> is presumably grammatically correct, but was not used to express 'my father'. As Radcliffe-Brown notes, '[in] *Aka-J̌eru* a man speaks of his father as *t'a-mai*' (RB$_2$: 66).

tobut (AKJ) *n*

Buttress root

Attestations:

(1) <Po̲ičotobut> '*Sterculia* buttress' (*pɔiʧo-tobut* 'buttress root of a *Sterculia* tree') (RB$_2$: 192)

Notes:

<Po̲ičotobut> is the name of the first ancestor who 'came out of the buttress of a *po̲ičo* (*Sterculia*) tree, and was called (...) *Sterculia* buttress' (RB$_2$: 192). We analyse this name as a noun-noun compound combining **pɔiʧo** with **tobut**.

tomo (AKJ, NA) *n*

1. Flesh

Attestations:

(1) <ê-chō-thômo> 'lap' (*e-ʧɔ tomo* 'flesh of the lap/thigh') (M: 171), <ê-chō-thōmo> 'thigh' (M: 172) (AKJ)

2. Wood

Attestations:

(1) <po̲ičo tomo> 'wood (literally flesh) of the *Sterculia* (*po̲ičo*) tree' (*pɔiʧo tomo* 'id.') (RB$_2$: 119) (NA)

Comparisons:

PGA *et*^{h}*omo* 'flesh, meat' (Abbi 2012: 351); Akachari <yetomó> [*sic*] 'flesh' (Portman 1887: 33)

Notes:

Cf. **etomo** and **ɛratomo**.

totemo (AKJ (?), NA) *n*

Kingfisher sp.

Attestations:

(1) <totemo> 'a species of kingfisher' (RB$_2$: 202) (AKJ (?))

(2) <totemo> [a species of kingfisher] (RB_2: 202) (NA)

Comparisons:
PGA *ʈoʈɛmo* 'bird' (Abbi 2012: 393); Akachari <Maia Totemo> 'Sir Kingfisher' (RB_2: 189, 202)

toto (AKJ, NA) *n*

1. Pandanus sp.

Attestations:
(1) <toto> 'species of *Pandanus*' (RB_2: 93) (NA)

2. Term of address for a girl during the initiation ceremony and for a short time afterwards

Attestations:
(1) <toto> 'girl [during the initiation ceremony and for a short time afterwards]' (RB_2: 93, 121) (NA)

Comparisons:
PGA *ʈɔʈɔ* 'pandanus' (Abbi 2012: 394), *toto 'Pandanus andamanensium* Kurz; *Pandanus leram* Jones' (Awasthi 1991: 279)

Notes:
'*Toto* is the name of the species of *Pandanus* from which women's belts are made and the leaves of which are used in the [initiation] ceremony' (RB_2: 93).

toto tɛrbua |toto t=Ø-ɛr-bua| (AKJ)
K.o. belt of pandanus leaf

Attestations:
(1) <toto t'er-bua> 'a belt of *Pandanus* leaf' (RB_2: 477), [a belt] (RB_2: 478)

Notes:
'Belts of this kind are generally worn by married women, but precisely similar belts are worn by men on certain ceremonial occasions' (RB_2: 477). The meaning of the noun <er-bua> is unclear. This word resembles the term for 'lip' recorded by Radcliffe-Brown as <îr-bôa> (cf. Akachari <ér buáh> 'lip'; Portman (1887: 47)).

toto tɛrmɔi |toto t=Ø-ɛr-mɔi| (AKJ)
K.o. girdle

Attestations:
(1) <toto t'er-mo̲i> 'kind of girdle' (RB_2: 478)

Notes:

'Yet another kind of girdle is made by splitting *Pandanus* leaves into thin strips and making them into a kind of wrapped cord, one strip being wrapped spirally round one or more others by the same technique as that used in making bow-strings. A number of coils of strands made in this way are tied together with thread at various points and a tassel similar to that of the *toto t'er-bua* is added at the back. Such girdles are usually improved by the addition of a few pendent strings of *Dentalium* shell. They may be worn by either men or women. Their name in Aka-Jeru is *toto t'er-mo̱i*' (RB$_2$: 478). The meaning of the noun <er-mo̱i> is obscure.

toto tɛrŋau |toto t=Ø-ɛr-ŋau| (AKJ)

K.o. girdle

Attestations:

(1) <toto t'er-ŋau> 'a girdle' (RB$_2$: 478)

Notes:

'Girdles are also made by cutting a number of strips of leaf and softening them by chewing them in the mouth. These strips are laid together and either served over or marled with thread so as to make a girdle of round section. A tassel of leaves similar to that of the *toto t'er-bua* is attached to the back, and very frequently strings of *Dentalium* shell are attached at various points. Such a girdle may be worn by either men or women. It is called *toto t'er-ŋau* in Aka-Jeru' (RB$_2$: 478). The meaning of the noun <er-ŋau> is obscure.

toto tɛrɲarab |toto t=Ø-ɛr-ɲarab| (AKJ)

K.o. belt

Attestations:

(1) <toto t'er-nyarab> 'a belt' (RB$_2$: 477)

Notes:

'A very similar belt is made in exactly the same way [as the **toto tɛrbua** – RZ/BC] save that the tassel of leaves at the back consists of narrow strips of Pandanus leaf instead of broad strips. This kind of belt is worn by women only. (...) It is called *toto t'er-nyarab* in Aka-Jeru' (RB$_2$: 477). The meaning of the noun <nyarab> is unknown.

toto tɛrapuli |toto t=Ø-ɛra-puli| (lit. 'pattern of the pandanus') (NA)

Pattern used to decorate a girl after the initiation ceremony

Attestations:

(1) <toto t'e̲ra-puli> 'pattern (...) used (...) to decorate a girl after the ceremony at her first menstruation' (RB$_2$: 124)

tɔi (AKJ, NA) *n*

1. Bone

Attestations:

(1) <to̲i> 'bone' (RB$_1$: 49), <ê-buròngo-tòi> 'rib' (*e-burɔŋo tɔi* 'bone of the side of the body') (M: 171) (AKJ)

(2) <to̲i> 'bone' (RB$_2$: 136, 137), <Lau to̲i> 'bones of a dead person' (RB$_2$: 137, 301) (NA)

2. Shell

Attestations:

(1) <ino ko̲lo to̲i> 'necklace of fresh-water shells' (*ino kɔlo tɔi* 'shells of a mollusc sp.') (RB$_2$: 480)

Comparisons:

PGA *etɔe* ~ *eʈoe* 'bone, backbone' (Abbi 2012: 351, 352), *oʈɔy* 'id.' (Abbi 2012: 377); Akachari <é toi í> 'id.' (Portman 1887: 213)

tɔkopɔr (AKJ) *n*

Cyclone

Attestations:

(1) <to̲ko-po̲r> 'cyclone' (RB$_2$: 352)

Notes:

Radcliffe-Brown indicates that this word literally means 'falling wood' or 'falling tree' (RB$_2$: 352), but neither a root meaning 'fall' nor a root meaning 'wood' or 'tree' can be recognised here.

tɔl (AKJ, NA) *n*

White clay

Attestations:

(1) <to̲l> 'white clay' (RB$_2$: 112), 'a fine white pipe-clay' (RB$_2$: 122) (AKJ)

(2) <to̲l> 'white clay' (RB$_2$: 111) (NA)

Comparisons:

PGA *ʈɔl* 'mud' (Abbi 2012: 393)

Notes:

Synonym: **tɔlodu**.

tɔlodu |tɔl-odu| (AKJ, NA) *n*

White clay

Attestations:

(1) <to̲l-odu> 'white clay' (RB$_2$: 112), 'a fine white pipe-clay' (RB$_2$: 122), 'fine white clay' (RB$_2$: 124) (AKJ)

(2) <to̲l-odu> 'white clay' (RB$_2$: 99, 102, 133, 180) (NA)

Comparisons:

PGA *toloḍu* 'clay' (Abbi 2012: 388); Akachari <tál ótó> 'white clay prepared' (Portman 1887: 213)

Synonym: **tɔl.**

tɔr (AKJ) *n*

K.o. bucket

Attestations:

(1) <tar> 'a bucket' (RB$_1$: 39), <ta̲r> 'bucket' (RB$_2$: 497, 498)

Comparisons:

PGA *tar* 'bucket' (Abbi 2012: 385); Akachari <tāūr> 'bucket' (Portman 1887: 155),

Notes:

See endnote 4 to Chapter 2.

tɔrodiu (NA) *n*

1. Full sun

Attestations:

(1) <to̲rodiu> 'sun' (RB$_2$: 141), <to̲ro-diu> 'the full sun' (RB$_2$: 144)

2. Middle part of the day

Attestations:

(1) <to̲ro-diu> 'middle part of the day when the sun is well up in the sky' (RB$_2$: 144)

Notes:

Cf. **diu**.

tɔrɔi (AKJ, NA) *n*

Bird sp.

Attestations:

(1) <to̲ro̲i> [a bird] (RB$_2$: 199) (AKJ)

(2) <to̲ro̲i> [a bird] (RB$_2$: 150, 156) (NA)

Comparisons:

Akabo (?), Akakhora <to̲ro̲i> [a bird] (RB$_2$: 199)

tɔrɔk (AKJ) *n*

Tree sp. (likely *Terminalia bialata*)

Attestations:

(1) <to̲ro̲k> [flower-name] (RB$_2$: 119)

Comparisons:

PGA *t̪orok* 'flower' (Abbi 2012: 392); Akachari <turok> 'Terminalia bialata' (Portman 1887: 220)

tɔrɔktato (NA) *n*

Tree sp.

Attestations:

(1) <to̲ro̲ktato> [a tree] (RB$_2$: 227)

tu |t-u| (NA) *pron*

(1) <t-u-boto-ba> 'I fell' (*t-u boto-ba* 'id.') (RB$_2$: 503)

Comparisons:

PGA *t̪*^{h}*u* '1SG' (Abbi 2013: 169); Akachari <tó> 'I' (Portman 1887: 115, 125, 129, 135, 145, 147, 149, 181, 189)

tuŋ (NA) *v*

To want

Attestations:

(1) <tio bi tuŋ-om> 'I want (I am wanting)' (*tio=bi tuŋ-om* 'id.') (RB$_2$: 503)

ʧaiɲo (AKJ, NA) *n*

Plant sp.

Attestations:

(1) <čainyo> 'a plant' (RB$_2$: 479) (AKJ)

(2) <čainyo> [a plant] (RB$_2$: 92, 93), 'a plant' (RB$_2$: 127, 479) (NA)

ʧarap (AKJ) *n*

Plant sp.

Attestations:

(1) <čarap> [flower-name] (RB$_2$: 119)

ʧari (NA) *n*

Salt water

Attestations:

(1) <čari> 'salt water' (RB$_2$: 24)

Comparisons:
PGA *sare* 'saline water, sea, salt' (Abbi 2012: 383); Akachari <chárií> 'salt, saline' (Portman 1887: 67), 'sea-water' (Portman 1887: 68)

Notes:
Cf. **akaʧari**.

ʧatlo (NA) *n*

1. Large star

Attestations:
(1) <čatlo> 'larger [star]' (RB_2: 141)

2. Beetle sp.

Attestations:
(1) <čatlo> 'a species of finely marked beetle' (RB_2: 141), 'a species of beetle' (RB_2: 156)

Comparisons:
PGA *cot̪lo* 'star' (Abbi 2012: 339)

ʧato (NA) *v*
To do, to make, to work

Attestations:
(1) <Biliku čatobom> 'Biliku is at work' (*biliku ʧato-bom* 'Biliku is working') (RB_2: 368), <Tarai čatobom> 'Tarai is at work' (*tarai ʧato-bom* 'Tarai is working') (RB_2: 368)

Comparisons:
PGA *cat̪o* 'to do, to work' (Abbi 2013: 113, 173, 210)

ʧelebi (AKJ) *n*
Plant sp. (likely *Diospyros densiflora*)

Attestations:
(1) <čelebi> [flower-name] (RB_2: 119)

Comparisons:
Akachari <chélebí> 'Diospyros densiflora'

ʧelene (NA) *n*
Bird sp.

Attestations:
(1) <čelene> [a bird] (RB_2: 150)

Comparisons:
PGA *cɛlene* 'little heron, *Buteroides striatus*' (Pande and Abbi 2011: 2), 'ruddy turnstone, *Arenaria interpres*' (Pande and Abbi: 28), *celene* 'bird, crab Plover' (Abbi 2012: 23, 337); Akabo (?) <čelene> [a bird] (RB_2: 199)

ʧelmo (AKJ, NA) *n*
Tree sp.: *Tetranthera lancifolia*

Attestations:
(1) <čelmo> '*Tetranthera* wood' (RB_2: 133) (AKJ)
(2) <čelmo> '*Tetranthera lancœfolia*' (RB_2: 92), 'Tetranthera' (RB_2: 102), '*Tetranthera* wood' (RB_2: 144) (NA)

Comparisons:
PGA *celmo* 'tree; flower' (Abbi 2012: 337); Akachari <chélmó> 'Tetranthera lancefolia' (Portman 1887: 229)

ʧeo (AKJ, NA) *n*
K.o. knife

Attestations:
(1) <čeo> 'a knife' (RB_1: 39) 'knife' (RB_2: 193) (AKJ)
(2) <čeo> 'a knife' (RB_2: 118) (NA)

Comparisons:
PGA *ceo* 'knife' (Abbi 2012: 338); Akachari <chéo> 'knife' (Portman 1887: 43), <chéó> 'iron knife' (Portman 1887: 207)

ʧereo (AKJ, NA) *n*
Bird sp.

Attestations:
(1) <čereo> [a bird] (RB_2: 199) (AKJ)
(2) <čereo> [a bird] (RB_2: 150) (NA)

Comparisons:
PGA *cɛreo* 'a type of Asian cuckoo' (Abbi 2012: 338); Akabo (?) <čereo> [a bird] (RB_2: 199)

ʧiba (AKJ, NA) *n*
Sling of bark for carrying children

Attestations:
(1) <čiba> 'a sling for carrying children' (RB_2: 39), 'bark sling' (RB_2: 76), 'sling used for carrying children' (RB_2: 128) (AKJ)
(2) <čiba> 'sling of bark used for carrying children' (RB_2: 90) (NA)

Comparisons:
PGA *ceba* 'sling' (Abbi 2012: 3); Akachari <chíbá> 'sling for carrying children' (Portman 1887: 209)

ʧirikli (AKJ) *n*
Moon

Attestations:
(1) <čirikli> 'moon' (RB_2: 142), <Maia Čirikli> 'id.' ('Sir Moon') (RB_2: 142)

Comparisons:
Akachari <chíríklí> 'moon' (Portman 1887: 191)

Notes:
RB_2 (p. 141) also records <dula> 'moon' as a NA form (cf. Akachari <dolāū> 'id.' (Portman 1887: 51) and <Maia Dula> 'moon' (lit. 'Sir Moon') (RB_2: 141)). PGA has *ɖulɔ* 'moon' (Abbi 2012: 342).

ʧiro (AKJ, NA) *n*
Liver (of an animal)

Attestations:
(1) <čokbi-čiro> 'turtle-liver' (RB_2: 101) (AKJ)
(2) <čokbi-čiro> 'turtle-liver' (RB_2: 119, 296) (NA)

Comparisons:
PGA *cokbiciro* 'liver of a turtle' (Abbi 2012: 338)

ʧo (NA) *n*
Plant sp. (likely *Entada pursœtha*)

Attestations:
(1) <čo> [a vegetable food] (RB_2: 199)

Comparisons:
PGA *co:* 'beans' (Abbi 2012: 338); Akachari <chāū> 'Entada pursœtha' (Portman 1887: 219)

ʧokbi (AKJ, NA) *n*
Turtle sp.

Attestations:
(1) <čokbi-čiro> 'turtle-liver' (*ʧokbi ʧiro* 'id.') (RB_2: 101), <čokbi-tei> 'turtle-blood' (*ʧokbi teo* 'id.') (RB_2: 498) (AKJ)
(2) <čokbi> 'turtle' (RB_2: 101, 118, 267), <čokbi-čiro> 'turtle-liver' (RB_2: 119, 296), <čokbi t'e̱ra-puli> 'turtle pattern' (*ʧokbi*

t=Ø-ɛra-puli 'pattern of the turtle') (RB_2: 123), <čokbi-tei> 'turtle-blood' (RB_2: 296) (NA)

Comparisons:
PGA *cokbi* 'green medium-sized turtle'; Akachari <chókbí> 'turtle'

ʧokbi kimil (NA) *n*
Turtle-eating ceremony

Attestations:
(1) <čokbi-kimil> 'turtle-eating ceremony' (RB_2: 101, 267)

Notes:
Synonym: **ʧokbiʤo**. Cf. **ʧokbi** and **kimil**.

ʧokbiʤo (NA) *n*
Turtle-eating ceremony

Attestations:
(1) <čokbi-ǰo> 'turtle-eating ceremony' (RB_2: 101, 267)

Notes:
'At the turtle-eating ceremony the youth is given a new name, of the nature of a nick-name' (RB_2: 120). Synonym: **ʧokbi kimil**. Cf. **ʧokbi** and **ʤo**.

ʧokoro (AKJ) *n*
Plant sp.

Attestations:
(1) <čokoro> [flower-name] (RB_2: 119)

Comparisons:
PGA *cɔkʰɔro* 'flower' (Abbi 2012: 339)

ʧoleke (AKJ) *n*
Tree sp.: *Pterocarpus dalbergioides*

Attestations:
(1) <čoleke> 'Pterocarpus tree' (RB_1: 39)

Comparisons:
PGA *cɔlekʰi* 'tree' (Abbi 2012: 339), *chawleke* 'Pterocarpus delbergoides [*sic*] Roxb.' (Awasthi 1991: 277); Akachari <choleké> 'Pterocarpus dalbergioides' (Portman 1887: 219)

ʧolmo (AKJ) *n*
Fish sp.: *Tetrodon* sp.

Attestations:

(1) <čolmo> 'a species of *Tetrodon*' (RB$_2$: 146)

ʧop (AKJ, NA) *n*

Tree sp. (likely *Terminalia* sp.)

Attestations:

(1) <čop> 'a species of tree' (RB$_2$: 101) (AKJ)
(2) <čop> 'a tree with edible nuts' (RB$_2$: 118) (NA)

Comparisons:

PGA *cɔp* 'tree; fruit' (Abbi 2012: 340); Akachari <chóp> 'Terminalia' (Portman 1887: 219), <chup> [*sic*] [fruit] (Portman 1887: 199)

ʧope (NA) *adj*

Many

Attestations:

(1) <renya čope> 'much baggage, many possessions' (RB$_2$: 119)

Comparisons:

PGA *cɔp^{h}e* 'many' (Abbi 2013: 114, 121, 122, 182, 190, 192, 246, 284, 286); Akachari <chópí> 'all, many' (Portman 1887: 157, 161)

ʧotɔt (AKJ, NA) *n*

Bird sp.

Attestations:

(1) <čoto̲t> [a bird] (RB$_2$: 199) (AKJ)
(2) <čoto̲t> [a bird] (RB$_2$: 150) (NA)

Comparisons:

PGA *cɔt̪ɔt̪* 'bird, partridge' (Abbi 2012: 340); Akabo (?) <čoto̲t> [a bird] (RB$_2$: 199)

ʧɔkʧura (AKJ (?)) *n*

Heron sp.

Attestations:

(1) <čo̲kčura> 'heron' (RB$_2$: 201, 202)

ʧɔm (NA) *n*

Palm sp. (probably *Areca catechu*)

Attestations:

(1) <čo̲m> 'Areca palm' (RB$_1$: 39), 'Areca' (RB$_2$: 222)

Comparisons:
PGA *cɔm* 'betelnut' (Abbi 2012: 339), *chom* '*Areca catechu* L.' (Awasthi 1991: 297); Akachari <chom> 'Areca laxa' (Portman 1887: 219)

ʧɔpʧura (AKJ, NA) *n*
Bird sp.

Attestations:
(1) <čo̱pčura> [a bird] (RB_2: 199) (AKJ)
(2) <co̱pcura> [a bird] (RB_2: 150) (NA)

ʧubi (AKJ) *n*
Snake

Attestations:
(1) <čubi> 'snake' (RB_1: 39, 40; RB_2: 497)

Comparisons:
PGA *ʃubi* ~ *subi* 'snake' (Abbi 2012: 384); Akachari <chubí> 'id.' (Portman 1887: 73, 168)

ʧuei (AKJ) *n*
Plant sp.

Attestations:
(1) <čuei> [a fruit] (RB_2: 142)

ʧugotɔ (AKJ) *n*
Tree sp.: *Mimusops indica*

Attestations:
(1) <čugoto> 'Mimusops tree' (RB_1: 39), <čugoto̱> 'Mimusops' (RB_2: 497)

Comparisons:
Akachari <chugotāū> 'Misopsus indica' (Portman 1887: 221)

ʧup (AKJ, NA) *n*
K.o. basket

Attestations:
(1) <čup> 'a basket' (RB_1: 39) (AKJ)
(2) <čup il> 'in the basket' (*ʧup=il* 'id.') (RB_2: 503) (NA)

Comparisons:
PGA *ʃup* ~ *sup* ~ *suːp* 'basket, bucket' (Abbi 2012: 14); Akachari <chup> 'id.'

ʧup tɔi (lit. 'bone of the basket') (NA)
Creeper sp.

Attestations:
(1) <čup-to̲i> 'a creeper' (RB_2: 465)

Notes:
The stem of this creeper is used to make baskets (RB_2: 465).

u |Ø-u| (NA) *pron*
He, she, it
(1) <u-ben-om> 'someone sleeping, he sleeping' (*Ø-u beno-m* 'He/she is sleeping') (RB_2: 501), 'sleeping' (RB_2: 503), <u-beno-ba> 'he slept or was sleeping' (*Ø-u beno-ba* 'id.') (RB_2: 504), <u-boto-ba> 'he or it fell' (*Ø-u boto-ba* 'id.') (RB_2: 504)

Comparisons:
PGA *u* '3SG' (Abbi 2013: 177); Akachari <u> 'he' (Portman 1887: 151, 163, 189)

8.2 English–Akajeru finder list

abdominal walls
Abdominal walls: *epilu* (AKJ)

ABSOLUTIVE
ABSOLUTIVE: $=bi_1$ (NA)

accompany
To accompany: *akaʧe* (NA)

adze
Adze: *olo* (AKJ)

after
After: *araiʧulu* (AKJ, NA)

afterwards
Afterwards: *taraiʧulik* (AKJ, NA)

Akachari
Akachari: *akaʧari* (NA)

Akajeru
Akajeru: *akaʤeru* (AKJ)

ALLATIVE
ALLATIVE: =*kak* (NA)

alone
Alone: *ʤutpu* (NA) (?)

ancestor
Ancestor: *lau tɛrkuro* (NA)
Ancestors: *akamai koloko* (NA)

anchor
Anchor: *ɛrameo* (AKJ)

angry

Angry: *tarendʒek* (NA) (?)

animal

A mythological animal that haunts the jungle: *dʒirmu* (NA)

ankle

Ankle: *oŋbrɔno* (AKJ)

arm

Arm: *ɛrkit* (AKJ)

armpit

Armpit: *oŋpoŋ* (AKJ)

ashamed

Ashamed: *otdʒete* (AKJ)

back

Back (n): *otbo* (AKJ, NA)

bad

Bad: *etʃai* (AKJ)

basket

K.o. basket: *tʃup* (AKJ, NA)

be

To be: =*bi*$_2$ (AKJ, NA)

be cold

To be cold: *ottau* (NA)

be hot

To be hot: *otkimil*$_2$ (NA)

be married

To marry, to be married: *ebui*$_2$ (NA)

beard

Beard: *ɛrtap betʃ* (AKJ)

beetle sp.

Beetle sp.: *tʃatlo* (NA)

belly

Belly: *itpet* (NA)

belt

K.o. belt: *toto tɛrɲarab* (AKJ)

K.o. belt of pandanus leaf: *toto tɛrbua* (AKJ)

K.o. belt of pandanus leaves worn by girls and women: *kudu* (AKJ)

big

Big: *ɛrkuro* (NA)

bird sp.

Bird sp.: *beɲe* (AKJ, NA)

Bird sp.: *biratkoro* (NA)

Bird sp.: *bobelo* (AKJ, NA)

Bird sp.: *kelil* (AKJ, NA)

Bird sp.: *milidu* (AKJ, NA)

Bird sp.: *mite*$_1$ (AKJ)

Bird sp.: *poruatɔko* (AKJ, NA)

Bird sp.: *taka* (AKJ)

Bird sp.: *tʃelene* (NA)

Bird sp.: *tʃɔptʃura* (AKJ, NA)

Bird sp.: *tɔrɔi* (AKJ, NA)

Bird sp.: *teo* (AKJ)

Bird sp.: *tʃereo* (AKJ, NA)

Bird sp.: *tʃotɔt* (AKJ, NA)

Green pigeon: *reŋko* (NA)

Heron sp.: *tʃɔktʃura* (AKJ (?))

Imperial pigeon: *mirid* (AKJ)

Kingfisher sp.: *lirtʃitmo* (AKJ)

Kingfisher sp.: *tiriɲ* (AKJ)

Kingfisher sp.: *tiritmo* (AKJ (?), NA)
Kingfisher sp.: *totemo* (AKJ (?), NA)
Oriole: *bani* (NA)
Rail: *mɔitʃo* (AKJ, NA)
Sea-eagle: *kɔlo* (AKJ, NA)

blood
Blood: *tei* (AKJ, NA)

bone
Bone: *tɔi* (AKJ, NA)
Bone of a dead person: *lau tɔi* (NA)

bowels
Intestines, bowels: *dʒekakɛt* (?) (AKJ)

boy
A boy after his back was scarified in an initiation ceremony: *edʒido* (NA)
A boy after his back was scarified in an initiation ceremony and before the turtle-eating ceremony: *okotaliŋ kolɔt* (NA)
A boy or girl during the turtle-eating ceremony or the pig-eating ceremony: *kimil* (AKJ, NA)
A boy or girl under certain ritual restrictions chiefly concerned with food: *akaop* (AKJ, NA)
A boy or girl who is passing through the initiation ceremonies: *akakimil kolɔt* (NA)

brother
One who has lost a brother or sister: *roputʃ* (AKJ, NA)

brother-in-law
Younger brother-in-law: *ebui otaraitʃulute* (NA)

bucket
K.o. bucket: *tɔr* (AKJ)

buttocks
Buttocks: *ɛratomo* (AKJ)

canoe
Canoe: *roa* (AKJ, NA)

catch hold
To catch hold: *nimi* (NA) (?)

cave
Cave: *ɛrapoŋ* (AKJ, NA)

centipede
Centipede: *terkobito* (NA)

ceremony
Turtle-eating ceremony: *kimildʒo* (NA), *tʃokbi kimil* (NA), *tʃokbidʒo* (NA)

cheek
Cheek: *ɛrnoko* (AKJ)

child
Child (non-possessed form): *etire*$_2$ (AKJ, NA)
Child (possessed form): *ottire* (NA)

cicada
Cicada: *mite*$_2$ (AKJ, NA)

clay
K.o. clay: *odu* (AKJ, NA)
White clay: *tɔl* (AKJ, NA), *tɔlodu* (AKJ, NA)

clothes
Clothes: *otʤulu*$_2$ (NA)

cold
Cold: *otʤulu*$_1$ (NA)
To be cold: *ottau* (NA)

COLLECTIVE
COLLECTIVE (for human nouns): *koloko* (NA)

come
To come and go: *elpe* (NA) (?)

condition
Condition of a boy or girl who is passing through the initiation ceremonies: *akakimil* (NA)
In the condition of having eaten certain foods: *otkimil*$_1$ (NA)

creek
Creek: *buliu* (AKJ)

creeper
Creeper: *balo* (NA)

creeper sp.
Creeper sp.: *bobi* (NA)
Creeper sp.: *korotli* (AKJ)
Creeper sp.: *ʧup tɔi* (NA)
Creeper sp.: *Pothos sandens*: *terkobito balo* (NA)

cyclone
Cyclone: tɔkopɔr (AKJ)

cyrena
Cyrena shell: *bun* (AKJ, NA)

dance
Having joined in a dance: *otkimil*$_1$ (NA)

daughter-in-law
Daughter-in-law: *otone* (NA)

day
Middle part of the day: *tɔrodiu* (NA)

DEFINITE ARTICLE
DEFINITE ARTICLE: *t=* (AKJ, NA)

die
To die: *empil* (NA)

do
To do, to make, to work: *ʧato* (NA)

dog
Dog: *bibi* (NA)

double of the sleeper
Double of the sleeper: *otʤumulo* (NA)

dream
Dream: *otʤumu*$_1$ (NA)
To dream: *otʤumu*$_2$ (NA)

dugong
Dugong: *kɔroin* (NA)

ear
Ear: *ɛrbuo* (AKJ)

eating
Eating, food: ʤo$_1$ (AKJ, NA)

enough
Enough: *deko* (NA)

eye
Eye: *ɛrulu* (AKJ)

eyebrow
Eyebrow: *ɛrulu betʃ* (AKJ)

eyelash
Eyelash: *ɛrulu totbetʃ* (AKJ)

face
Face: *ɛrmiku* (AKJ)

fall
To fall: *boto* (NA)

father
Father: *akamai* (AKJ, NA)

father-in-law
Father-in-law: *epotatʃiu* (NA)

female
Female: *buku* (NA)

fever
Fever: *etei*$_1$ (NA)

finger
Finger: *oŋkɔra* (AKJ)

finish
To finish: *ɛralio* (NA)

firefly
Firefly: *kataɲ* (AKJ)

fish sp.
Fish sp.: *bol*$_1$ (NA)
Fish sp.: *komar* (AKJ, NA)
Fish sp.: *Plotosus* sp.: *ɲuri* (NA)
Fish sp.: *Tetrodon* sp.: *tʃolmo* (AKJ)

flesh
Flesh: *tomo* (AKJ, NA)
Flesh of the body, meat: *etomo* (AKJ)

fly sp.
Fly sp.: *pulimu* (NA)

foam
Foam on a rough sea: *air* (AKJ)

follow
To follow: *araitʃulutu* (AKJ, NA)

food
Eating, food: *ʤo*$_1$ (AKJ, NA)
K.o. vegetable food: *bui* (NA)

foot
Foot: *oŋmatɔ* (AKJ)

forearm
Forearm: *ɛrbala* (AKJ)
Fleshy portion of the forearm: *oŋba* (AKJ)

forehead
Forehead: *ɛrmiku* (AKJ)

forest
Forest, jungle: *timiku* (NA)

frog sp.
Frog sp.: *bɛrɛt* (NA)
Frog sp.: *pɔrubi* (NA)

fruit
Fruit: *ottʃo* (AKJ, NA)

girdle
K.o. girdle: *toto tɛrmɔi* (AKJ)
K.o. girdle: *toto tɛrŋau* (AKJ)

girl
A boy or girl under certain ritual restrictions chiefly concerned with food: *akaop* (AKJ, NA)
A boy or girl during the turtle-eating ceremony or the pig-eating ceremony: *kimil* (AKJ, NA)
A boy or girl who is passing through the initiation ceremonies: *akakimil kolɔt* (NA)
A girl between the ceremony that takes place on the occasion of her first menstrual discharge: *akandu kolɔt* (NA)
Term of address for a girl during the initiation ceremony and for a short time afterwards: *alebe* (NA), *toto* (AKJ, NA)

good
Good: *enol* (AKJ, NA)

grandfather
Maternal grandfather: *akamimi akamai* (AKJ, NA)

green pigeon
Green pigeon: *reŋko* (NA)

hair
Hair: *betʃ* (AKJ), *otbetʃ* (NA)
Head hair: *ɛrbetʃ* (AKJ)

hand
Hand: *oŋkɔra* (AKJ, NA) ~ *oŋkɔro* (NA)

have in adoption
To have in adoption: *oitʃolo* (NA)

he
He, she, it: *io* (AKJ, NA), *u* (NA)

head
Head: *ottʃo* (AKJ, NA)
Head, skull: *ɛrtʃo* (AKJ, NA)

headache
Headache: *ottei* (AKJ)

heart
Heart (seat of affections): *ɛrtʃar* (AKJ)

her
His, hers, her: *itʃo* (NA)

heron sp.
Heron sp.: *tʃɔktʃura* (AKJ (?))

hers
His, hers, her: *itʃo* (NA)

high-tide
High-tide: *piletʃar* (AKJ)

his
His, hers, her: *itʃo* (NA)

honey
Black honey: *maro* (NA)

hot
Hot: *ɛrkimil* (NA)
To be hot: *otkimil*$_2$ (NA)

husband
Husband, wife: *ebui*$_1$ (NA)

I
I: *t=* (AKJ, NA), *tio* (AKJ, NA), *tu* (NA)

imperial pigeon
Imperial pigeon: *mirid* (AKJ)

INESSIVE
INESSIVE: *=ko* (NA) (?)

insect sp.
Beetle sp.: *tʃatlo* (NA)
Centipede: *terkobito* (NA)
Cicada: *mite*$_2$ (AKJ, NA)
Firefly: *kataɲ* (AKJ)
Fly sp.: *pulimu* (NA)
Insect sp.: *reo* (NA)
Spider: *biliku* (NA)

intestines
Intestines, bowels: *ʤekakɛt* (AKJ) (?)

iron
Iron: *remu* (NA)

it
He, she, it: *io* (AKJ, NA), *u* (NA)

jaw
Lower jaw: *ɛrtap* (AKJ)

jungle
Forest, jungle: *timiku* (NA)

kingfisher sp.
Kingfisher sp.: *lirtʃitmo* (AKJ)
Kingfisher sp.: *tiriɲ* (AKJ)
Kingfisher sp.: *tiritmo* (AKJ (?), NA)
Kingfisher sp.: *totemo* (AKJ (?), NA)

knife
K.o. knife: *tʃeo* (AKJ, NA)

knuckle
Knuckle: *oŋkide* (AKJ), *oŋkuʤu* (AKJ)

lady
Lady: *mimi* (AKJ, NA)

lap
Lap, thigh: *etʃɔ* (AKJ)

leaf
Leaf: *tetʃ* (NA)

Palm leaf (*Licuala* sp.): *kɔbo* (AKJ)

lightning
Lightning: *ele* (AKJ)

light-skinned person
Light-skinned person (European or Asian): *lau* (NA)

lip
Lip: *ɛrboa* (AKJ)

liver
Liver (of a an animal): *ʧiro* (AKJ, NA)

LOCATIVE
LOCATIVE: *=il* (NA)

long
Long, tall: *ɛralobuŋ* (AKJ), *elobuŋ* (AKJ)

make
To do, to make, to work: *ʧato* (NA)

make a torch of
To make a torch of: *moiʧ* (NA)

male
Male: *taru* (NA)
Man, male: *etaru* (NA)

man
Man, male: *etaru* (NA)

mangrove sp.
Mangrove sp.: *kabal* (NA)

many
Many: *ʧope* (NA)

marry
To marry, to be married: *ebui*$_2$ (NA)

mat
Sleeping mat: *baraba* (AKJ)

me
Me: *t=* (AKJ, NA)

meat
Flesh of the body, meat: *etomo* (AKJ)

medicine-man
Medicine-man: *okoʤumu* (AKJ, NA)

mine
Mine, my: *tiʧo* (AKJ, NA)

mist
Mist: *milite* (NA)

mister
Sir, mister: *mai* (AKJ, NA) ~ *maya* (AKJ, NA)

mollusc sp.
Mollusc sp.: *ino kɔlo* (AKJ)

moon
Moon: *ʧirikli* (AKJ)

mother
Mother: *akamimi* (AKJ, NA), *itpet* (NA)

mother-in-law
Mother-in-law: *epotatʃip* (NA)

mother-of-pearl
Mother-of-pearl shell: *be* (AKJ, NA)

mourner
Mourner: *akaodu* (NA)

mouth
Mouth: *akapoŋ* (AKJ)

mushroom sp.
mushroom sp.: *pata* (NA) (?)

my
Mine, my: *titʃo* (AKJ, NA)

nail
Nail (of finger or toe): *oŋkara* (AKJ)

navel
Navel: *eŋet* (AKJ)

neck
Neck: *otloŋo* (AKJ)

necklace
Necklace of fresh-water shells: *ino kɔlo tɔi* (AKJ)

needle
Netting needle: *kutobi* (AKJ)

NEGATIVE
NEGATIVE: *pu* (NA)

nephew
Nephew, niece (child of an older brother or sister): *ototoatue ottire* (NA)

nest
Nest of the white ants: *kɔt* (AKJ)

new
New (of the moon): *etire*$_1$ (NA)

niece
Nephew, niece (child of an older brother or sister): *ototoatue ottire* (NA)

night
Night: *bat* (NA)

nose
Nose: *ɛrkɔto* (AKJ)

offspring
Offspring of an animal (non-possessed form): *etire*$_2$ (AKJ, NA)

oriole
Oriole: *bani* (NA)

orphan
Orphan: *bolok* (AKJ, NA)

palm of the hand
Palm of the hand: *oŋkɔtra* (AKJ)

palm sp.
Palm sp. (probably *Areca catechu*): *tʃɔm* (NA)

Palm sp.: *Calamus* sp.: *pir* (AKJ)
Palm sp.: *Calamus tigrinus*: *bido* (NA)
Palm sp.: *Caryota mitis*: *pɔrɔto* (AKJ)
Palm sp.: *Licuala* sp.: *kɔbo* (AKJ, NA)

palm-leaf fibre
Shredded palm-leaf fibre: *kɔro* (AKJ, NA)

pandanus sp.
Pandanus sp.: *toto* (AKJ, NA)

pattern
Pattern in painting a person ornamentally: *ɛrapuli* (AKJ, NA)
Pattern of zig-zag lines painted on the body with white clay: *ɔrtʃubi tɛrabat* (AKJ, NA)
Pattern used to decorate a boy or a girl after the initiation ceremony: *kimil tɛrapuli* (NA)

person of the same generation
Older person of the same generation: *otareupu* (NA), *ototoatue* (NA)
Younger person of the same generation: *arabela* (NA), *araitʃulute* (AKJ, NA), *aralitʃu* (NA)

photograph
Photograph: *otdʒumulo* (NA)

piece
Piece of iron: *remu tɔi* (NA)

pig
Pig: *ra* (AKJ, NA)

pigeon
Green pigeon: *reŋko* (NA)
Imperial pigeon: *mirid* (AKJ)

pigment
A red pigment: *keip* (AKJ)

place
Place: *ti* (AKJ)

plant sp.
Creeper: *balo* (NA)
Creeper sp.: *bobi* (NA)
Creeper sp.: *korotli* (AKJ)
Creeper sp.: *tʃup tɔi* (NA)
Creeper sp.: *Pothos sandens*: *terkobito balo* (NA)
Mangrove sp.: *kabal* (NA)
Mushroom sp.: *pata* (NA) (?)
Palm sp. (probably *Areca catechu*): *tʃɔm* (NA)
Palm sp.: *Calamus* sp.: *pir* (AKJ)
Palm sp.: *Calamus tigrinus*: *bido* (NA)
Palm sp.: *Caryota mitis*: *pɔrɔto* (AKJ)
Palm sp.: *Licuala* sp.: *kɔbo* (AKJ, NA)
Pandanus sp.: *toto* (AKJ, NA)
Plant sp.: *bɔtek* (AKJ)
Plant sp.: *burut* (AKJ)
Plant sp.: *deŋ* (AKJ)
Plant sp.: *dʒili* (AKJ, NA)
Plant sp.: *dʒin* (AKJ)
Plant sp.: *mit* (AKJ)
Plant sp.: *mukui* (AKJ)

Plant sp.: *okɔr* (AKJ)
Plant sp.: *pare* (AKJ)
Plant sp.: *re* (AKJ)
Plant sp.: *ʧaiɲo* (AKJ, NA)
Plant sp.: *ʧarap* (AKJ)
Plant sp. (likely *Diospyros densiflora*): *ʧelebi* (AKJ)
Plant sp. (likely *Entada pursœtha*): *ʧo* (NA)
Plant sp.: *ʧokoro* (AKJ)
Plant sp.: *ʧuei* (AKJ)
Plant sp.: *Mucuna* sp.: *buyo* (NA)
Tree sp.: *piɲ* (AKJ (?))
Tree sp.: *tare* (AKJ)
Tree sp.: *tip* (AKJ)
Tree sp. (likely *Terminalia bialata*): *tɔrɔk* (AKJ)
Tree sp.: *tɔrɔktato* (NA)
Tree sp. (likely *Terminalia* sp.): *ʧop* (AKJ, NA)
Tree sp.: *Dipterocarpus laevis*: *kɔrɔin* (AKJ)
Tree sp.: *Erythrina orientalis*: *laro* (AKJ)
Tree sp.: *Ficus laccifera*: *reŋo* (AKJ, NA)
Tree sp.: *Hibiscus tiliaceus*: *bol*$_2$ (NA)
Tree sp.: *Mimusops indica*: *ʧugotɔ* (AKJ)
Tree sp.: *Myristica longifolia*: *poramo* (NA)
Tree sp.: *Pterocarpus dalbergioides*: *ʧoleke* (AKJ)
Tree sp.: *Sterculia* sp.: *ʤeru* (AKJ, NA)
Tree sp.: *Sterculia* sp.: *mɔyo* (AKJ)
Tree sp.: *Sterculia macrophylla*: *pɔiʧo* (AKJ, NA)
Tree sp.: *Terminalia procera*: *puliu* (AKJ)
Tree sp.: *Tetranthera lancifolia*: *ʧelmo* (AKJ, NA)
Yam sp.: *Dioscorea* sp.: *kɔnmo* (NA)
Yam sp.: *Dioscorea* sp.: *mino* (NA)

Port Blair
Port Blair: *lau taraɲu* (AKJ), *lautiʧe* (NA)

possessions
Possessions: *reɲa* (NA)

pot
Pot: *peʧ* (AKJ, NA)

prawn sp.
Prawn sp.: *dik* (NA)

prow
Prow of a canoe: *roa totʧo* (AKJ)

rail
Rail: *mɔiʧo* (AKJ, NA)

rain
Rain: *ʤiʧɛr* (NA)

rainbow
Rainbow: *pir* (AKJ)

rainy season
A brief period of unsettled weather at the end of the rainy season: *kimil* (AKJ, NA)

reel
Reel used in rope-making: *kutobi* (AKJ)

reflection
Reflection: *otʤumulo* (NA)

resin
K.o. resin: *biu* (NA)

rib
Rib: *eburoŋo tɔi* (AKJ)

rope
Rope: *luremo* (NA)

root
Buttress root: *tobut* (AKJ)
K.o. root: *ʤi* (AKJ)
K.o. root: *labo* (AKJ)
K.o. root: *lɔito* (AKJ)
K.o. root: *mikulu* (AKJ)

say
To tell, to say: *akarka* (AKJ)

sea-eagle
Sea-eagle: *kɔlo* (AKJ, NA)

shadow
Shadow: *otʤumulo* (NA)

she
He, she, it: *io* (AKJ, NA), *u* (NA)

shell
Cyrena shell: *bun* (AKJ, NA)
Mother-of-pearl shell: *be* (AKJ, NA)
Shell: *tɔi* (AKJ, NA)

shoulder
Shoulder: *ɛrkum* (AKJ)

shoot of a plant
Young shoot of a plant: *ɛratire* (AKJ, NA)

shy
Shy: *otʤete* (AKJ)

side of the body
Side of the body: *eburɔŋo* (AKJ)

sing
To sing: *eur* (NA)

sir
Sir, mister: *mai* (AKJ, NA) ~ *maya* (AKJ, NA)

sister
One who has lost a brother or sister: *roputʃ* (AKJ, NA)

skull
Head, skull: *ɛrtʃo* (AKJ, NA)
Skull of a dead person: *lau tɛrtʃo* (NA)

sky
Sky: *tau* (AKJ, NA)
'Lapidary sky': *tau meo* (NA)

sleep
To sleep: *beno* (NA)

sling
Sling of bark for carrying children: *tʃiba* (AKJ, NA)

small
Small: *eleo* (NA)

snake
Snake: *tʃubi* (AKJ)

snake sp.
Snake sp.: *Ophiophagus elaps*: *ɔrtʃubi* (AKJ, NA)

sole
Sole of the foot: *oŋkɔtra* (AKJ)

song
Song: *ʤo$_2$* (NA)

son-in-law
Son-in-law: *otone* (NA)

space under
Space under: *aramiku* (AKJ, NA)

spider
Spider: *biliku* (NA)

spine
Spine: *omrap* (AKJ)

spirit
Sea spirit: *ʤurua* (NA)
Spirit: *lau* (NA)
Spirit of the *Calamus* leaf: *bido tetʃ lau* (NA)
Spirit of the forest: *timiku lau* (NA)

star
Large star: *tʃatlo* (NA)
Small star: *kataɲ* (AKJ)

stone
K.o. soft red stone: *talar* (NA)
Stone: *meo* (AKJ, NA)

storm
Storm (?): *piribi* (AKJ) (?)

strong
Strong: *otlam* (NA)

structure
Structure erected across a dancing ground: *kɔrotʃop* (NA)

sun
Full sun: *tɔrodiu* (NA)
Sun: *diu* (AKJ, NA)

supernatural being
A female supernatural being: *biliku* (AKJ, NA)
A male supernatural being: *tarai* (AKJ, NA)

tail
Tail (of snake or turtle): *ɛrabat* (AKJ, NA)

talk
To talk: *ar* (NA)

tall
Long, tall: *elobuŋ* (AKJ), *ɛralobuŋ* (AKJ)

tell
To tell, to say: *akarka* (AKJ)

there
There (distant): *kulel* (AKJ, NA)

they
They: *n=* (NA), *nio* (AKJ, NA), *nu* (NA)

thigh

Lap, thigh: *etʃɔ* (AKJ)

this

This: *kidi* (NA)

throat

Throat: *akanɔro* (AKJ)

thunder

Thunder: *korude* (NA)

tongue

Tongue: *akatat* (AKJ)

tooth

Tooth: *ɛrpile* (AKJ)

torch

Torch of resin: *biumɔitʃ* (NA)

tree sp.

Mangrove sp.: *kabal* (NA)
Palm sp. (probably *Areca catechu*): *tʃɔm* (NA)
Palm sp.: *Caryota mitis*: *pɔrɔto* (AKJ)
Palm sp.: *Licuala* sp.: *kɔbo* (AKJ, NA)
Tree sp.: *piɲ* (AKJ (?))
Tree sp.: *tare* (AKJ)
Tree sp.: *tip* (AKJ)
Tree sp. (likely *Terminalia bialata*): *tɔrɔk* (AKJ)
Tree sp.: *tɔrɔktato* (NA)
Tree sp. (likely *Terminalia* sp.): *tʃop* (AKJ, NA)
Tree sp.: *Dipterocarpus laevis*: *kɔrɔin* (AKJ)
Tree sp.: *Erythrina orientalis*: *laro* (AKJ)
Tree sp.: *Ficus laccifera*: *reŋo* (AKJ, NA)
Tree sp.: *Hibiscus tiliaceus*: *bol$_2$* (NA)
Tree sp.: *Mimusops indica*: *tʃugotɔ* (AKJ)
Tree sp.: *Myristica longifolia*: *poramo* (NA)
Tree sp.: *Pterocarpus dalbergioides*: *tʃoleke* (AKJ)
Tree sp.: *Sterculia* sp.: *ʤeru* (AKJ, NA)
Tree sp.: *Sterculia* sp.: *mɔyo* (AKJ)
Tree sp.: *Sterculia macrophylla*: *pɔitʃo* (AKJ, NA)
Tree sp.: *Terminalia procera*: *puliu* (AKJ)
Tree sp.: *Tetranthera lancifolia*: *tʃelmo* (AKJ, NA)

turn in one's sleep

To turn in one's sleep (?): *kea* (NA) (?)

turtle sp.

Turtle sp.: *tʃokbi* (AKJ, NA)

uncle

Younger paternal uncle: *akamai otaraitʃulute* (NA)

urine

Urine: *araket* (AKJ)

village

Village: *araɲu* (NA)

walk

To walk backwards and forwards, to wander: *kiʤeri* (NA)

wander
To walk backwards and forwards, to wander: *kiʤeri* (NA)

want
To want: *tuŋ* (NA)

water
Fresh water: *ino* (AKJ, NA)
Salt water: *ʧari* (NA)
Water: *ino* (AKJ, NA)

we
We: *m=* (NA), *mio* (AKJ)

whiskers
Whiskers: *ɛrnoko beʧ* (AKJ)

who
Who: *aʧiu* (AKJ)

wife
Husband, wife: *ebui*$_1$ (NA)

wind
North-east wind: *biliku bɔto* (AKJ, NA)
South-west wind: *tarai bɔto* (AKJ, NA)
Wind: *bɔto* (AKJ, NA)

woman
Older woman of the same generation: *otarepʧip* (NA), *ototoatueʧip* (NA)
Woman: *ebuku* (NA)
Younger woman of the same generation: *araiʧuluteʧip* (NA)

wood
Wood: *tomo* (AKJ, NA)

work
To do, to make, to work: *ʧato* (NA)

world
World of the spirits that lies under this one: *maramiku* (NA)

wrestle
To wrestle: *bɔiʧo* (NA) (?)

wrist
Wrist: *oŋtɔi* (AKJ)

yam sp.
Yam sp.: *Dioscorea* sp.: *kɔnmo* (NA)
Yam sp.: *Dioscorea* sp.: *mino* (NA)

yesterday
Yesterday: *tɛraiʧiro* (AKJ)

you
You (pl.): *ŋil=* (NA), *ŋilio* (AKJ, NA)
You (sg.): *ŋ=* (NA), *ŋio* (AKJ, NA)

Appendix
Sources of examples (1)–(123)

(1) RB_1: 39, M: 169, RB_2: 142, RB_2: 193, RB_1: 49, RB_2: 497, RB_1: 39, RB_1: 39, M: 169 — (2) RB_2: 500, RB_2: 499, RB_2: 500, RB_2: 499 — (3) M: 171, 172, RB_2: 498, RB_2: 500 — (4*a*) RB_2: 39, RB_2: 101 — (4*b*) RB_2: 101, RB_2: 267 — (5) RB_2: 166, RB_2: 166, 167 — (6) RB_1: 39, RB_2: 91 — (7) RB_2: 193, RB_2: 504 — (8) RB_2: 500, RB_2: 501, RB_2: 66–7, RB_2: 501 — (9*a*) RB_2: 23, M: 171, M: 171, M: 170 — (9*b*) RB_2: 499, RB_2: 497, RB_2: 101, RB_2: 137 — (9*c*) RB_2: 501, RB_2: 501, RB_2: 503, RB_2: 504 — (9*d*) RB_2: 500 — (10*a*) M: 170, M: 170 — (10*b*) RB_1: 49, M: 172 — (11*a*) RB_2: 119, RB_2: 24 — (11*b*) RB_2: 500, RB_2: 500 — (11*c*) RB_1: 39, RB_2: 111 — (11*d*) RB_2: 24, RB_2: 24 — (12*a*) RB_2: 65, RB_2: 54 — (12*b*) RB_2: 133, RB_2: 54 — (12*c*) RB_2: 48, RB_2: 166 — (13) RB_2: 23, M: 172 — (14) M: 172 — (15) RB_2: 24, RB_2: 24 — (16) RB_2: 94, RB_2: 111, RB_2: 101 — (17) RB_2: 54, RB_2: 54, RB_2: 501 — (18) RB_2: 54, RB_2: 66 — (19) M: 172, RB_2: 500 — (20) RB_2: 500 — (21) RB_2: 124 — (22) RB_2: 56, RB_2: 66, 67 — (23) RB_2: 192–3 — (24) RB_2: 500, RB_2: 501 — (25) RB_2: 503 — (26) RB_2: 500, RB_2: 500 — (27) RB_2: 137, RB_2: 500, RB_2: 500 — (28) M: 171, RB_2: 500, RB_2: 499 — (29) M: 171, M: 169, M: 171 — (30) RB_2: 499, RB_2: 499, RB_2: 124, RB_2: 54, RB_2: 54, RB_2: 290 — (31) RB_2: 499, RB_2: 500, RB_2: 497, RB_2: 498 — (32) RB_2: 503 — (33) M: 171, M: 170, M: 170, M: 171, M: 170, M: 171, M: 172, M: 169 — (34) M: 169, M: 169, M: 170 — (35) M: 170, M: 170 — (36) M: 170, RB_2: 45, RB_2: 101 — (37) M: 170, M: 170, M: 171, M: 171, M: 171, M: 172, M: 169 — (38) M: 169, M: 169 — (39) M: 172 — (40) RB_2: 498, 499, RB_2: 499, RB_2: 119, M: 171 — (41) RB_2: 55, RB_2: 55 — (42) RB_2: 56, RB_2: 66–7, RB_2: 56, RB_2: 56, RB_2: 54 — (43) RB_2: 54, RB_2: 54 — (44) M: 169 — (45) RB_2: 81 — (46) RB_2: 166 — (47) RB_2: 166 — (48) RB_2: 498, RB_2: 266, 267, RB_2: 138, RB_2: 504 — (49) RB_2: 48, RB_2: 95 — (50) RB_2: 290, 499 — (51) RB_2: 501, RB_2: 500 — (52) Abbi (2012: 386), Abbi (2012: 386), Abbi (2012: 387) — (53) RB_2: 54 — (54) RB_2: 54, RB_2: 55, RB_2: 54, RB_2: 54 — (55*a*) RB_2: 501, RB_2: 504,

RB_2: 501 — (55*b*) RB_2: 55, RB_2: 54 — (56) Abbi (2013: 183) — (57) Portman (1887: 165) — (58) RB_2: 504 — (59) RB_2: 501 — (60) RB_2: 24 — (61) RB_2: 267 — (62) RB_2: 55 — (63) RB_2: 504 — (64) RB_2: 504 — (65) Abbi (2013: 172) — (66) RB_2: 504 — (67) RB_2: 54 — (68) RB_2: 500 — (69) RB_2: 137 — (70) RB_2: 504 — (71) Radcliffe-Brown (1922: 497) (not in RB_2) — (72) RB_2: 499 — (73) RB_2: 137 — (74) Abbi (2013: 122) — (75) Abbi (2013: 132) — (76) RB_2: 503 — (77) RB_2: 504 — (78) RB_2: 503 — (79) RB_2: 503 — (80) RB_2: 503 — (81) Portman (1887: 149) — (82) Abbi (2013: 260) — (83) Portman (1887: 135) — (84) Abbi (2013: 264) — (85) RB_2: 134 — (86) RB_2: 99 — (87) RB_2: 112 — (88) RB_2: 101 — (89) RB_2: 101 — (90) RB_2: 136 — (91) RB_2: 136 — (92) RB_2: 480 — (93) RB_2: 504 — (94) RB_2: 136 — (95) RB_2: 101 — (96) RB_2: 124 — (97) RB_2: 144 — (98*a*) RB_2: 66 — (98*b*) RB_2: 54 — (99) RB_2: 503 — (100) RB_2: 503 — (101) RB_2: 503 — (102) RB_2: 119 — (103) RB_2: 504 — (104) Radcliffe-Brown (1922: 497) (not in RB_2) — (105) RB_2: 503 — (106) RB_2: 190 — (107) RB_2: 119 — (108) RB_2: 124 — (109) RB_2: 89 — (110) RB_2: 55 — (111) RB_2: 192–3 — (112) RB_2: 119 — (113) RB_2: 296 — (114) RB_2: 137 — (115) RB_2: 119 — (116) M: 169 — (117) RB_2: 119 — (118) RB_2: 201, 45, 55 — (119) RB_2: 147 — (120) RB_2: 502 — (121) RB_2: 501 — (122) RB_2: 267 — (123) RB_2: 503

References

Abbi, Anvita. 2006. *Endangered Languages of the Andaman Islands*. Munich: Lincom Europa.

Abbi, Anvita. 2012. *Dictionary of the Great Andamanese Language: English-Great Andamanese-Hindi*. Delhi: Ratna Sagar.

Abbi, Anvita. 2013. *A Grammar of the Great Andamanese Language: An ethnolinguistic study*. Leiden and Boston: Brill.

Abbi, Anvita. 2020. 'The pandemic also threatens endangered languages', *Scientific American Blogs*. Accessed 31 March 2021. https://blogs.scientificamerican.com/voices/the-pandemic-also-threatens-endangered-languages/.

Avtans, Abhishek. 2006. 'Deictic categories in Great Andamanese'. MPhil dissertation, Jawaharlal Nehru University, New Delhi.

Awasthi, A. K. 1991. 'Ethnobotanical studies of the Negrito Islanders of Andaman Islands, India: the Great Andamanese', *Economic Botany* 45: 274–80.

Basu, Dwijendra N. 1952. 'A linguistic introduction to Andamanese', *Department of Anthropology Bulletin (Delhi)* 1/2: 55–70.

Bonington, M. C. C. 1932. *Census of India, 1931*. Vol. 2: *The Andaman and Nicobar Islands*. Calcutta: Government of India, Central Publication Branch.

Chattopadhyay, Madhumala. 2003. 'Quest for survival of the Negrito tribes of Andaman: the Great Andamanese, the Onge, the Jarawa, and the Sentinelese'. In *Tribal Development in Andaman Islands*, edited by A. N. Sharma, 59–80. New Delhi: Sarup & Sons.

Choudhary, Narayan K. 2006. 'Developing a computational framework for the verb morphology of Great Andamanese'. MPhil dissertation, Jawaharlal Nehru University, New Delhi.

Comrie, Bernard and Raoul Zamponi. 2017. 'Typological profile of the Great Andamanese family', *Journal of South Asian Languages and Linguistics* 4: 55–83.

Comrie, Bernard and Raoul Zamponi. 2019. 'Subgrouping and lexical distance in the Great Andamanese family'. In *Wortschätze und Sprachwelten: Beiträge zu Sprachtypologie, kontrastiver Wort- bzw. Wortschatzforschung und Pragmatik*, edited by Michail L. Kotin, 35–57. Berlin: Peter Lang.

Cooper, Zarine. 2002. *Archaeology and History: Early settlements in the Andaman Islands*. New Delhi and Oxford: Oxford University Press.

Dasgupta, Dipankar and S. R. Sharma. 1982. *A Hand Book [sic] of Onge Language*. Calcutta: Anthropological Survey of India.

Dixon, R. M. W. 1982. *Where Have All the Adjectives Gone? And other essays in semantics and syntax*. Berlin/New York/Amsterdam: Mouton.

Dixon, R. M. W. 2004. 'Adjective classes in typological perspective'. In *Adjective Classes: A cross-linguistic typology*, edited by R. M. W. Dixon and Alexandra Y. Aikhenvald, 1–49. Oxford: Oxford University Press.

Ganguly, Pranab. 1972 [1966]. 'Vocabulary of the Negritos of Little Andaman with grammatical notes and materials', *Bulletin of the Department of Anthropology* 15: 1–30.

Gudschinsky, Sarah C. 1956. 'The ABC's of lexicostatistics', *Word* 12: 175–210.

Heine-Geldern, Robert von. 1963. 'Archaeology and legend in the Andaman Islands'. In *Festschrift Paul Schebesta zum 75. Geburtstag, gewidmet von Mitbrüdern, Freunden und Schülern*, edited by Anton Vorbichler and Wilhelm Dupre, 129–32. Vienna/Mödling: St. Gabriel-Verlag.

Jenner, Philip N. 2009. *A Dictionary of Pre-Angkorian Khmer*. Edited by Doug Cooper. Canberra: The Australian National University.

Kumar, Chandan. 2001. 'Speech sounds in Andamanese: a descriptive study'. MPhil dissertation, Jawaharlal Nehru University, New Delhi.

Kumar, Pramod. 2012. 'Descriptive and typological study of Jarawa'. PhD thesis, Jawaharlal Nehru University, New Delhi.

Local Gazetteer. 1908. *The Andaman and Nicobar Islands*. Calcutta: Superintendent Government Printing.

Lowis, R. F. 1912. *Census of India, 1911*. Vol. 2: *The Andaman and Nicobar Islands*. Calcutta: Superintendent Government Printing.

Lowis, R. F. 1923. *Census of India, 1921*. Vol. 2: *The Andaman and Nicobar Islands*. Calcutta: Superintendent Government Printing.

Man, Edward H. 1919–23. 'Dictionary of the South Andaman language', *Indian Antiquary* 48 (1919) Supp. 1–84, 49 (1920) Supp. 85–136, 50 (1921) Supp. 137–64, 51 (1922) Supp. 165–88, 52 (1923) Supp. 189–203.

Man, Edward H. 1923. *A Dictionary of the South Andaman (Âkà-Bêa) Language with Grammatical Notes, Map, Illustrations and Several Appendices*. Bombay: British India Press.

Manoharan, S. 1989. *A Descriptive and Comparative Study of the Andamanese Language*. Calcutta: Anthropological Survey of India.

Manoharan, S. 1997. 'Pronominal prefixes and formative affixes in Andamanese language'. In *Languages of Tribal and Indigenous Peoples of India: The ethnic space*, edited by Anvita Abbi, 457–73. Delhi: Motilal Banarsidass.

Manoharan, S. and V. Gnanasundaram. 2007. *Linguistic Identity of an Endangered Tribe: Present Great Andamanese (Andaman and Nicobar Islands – India)*. Mysore: Central Institute of Indian Languages.

Mohanty, P. K. 2006. *Encyclopaedia of Scheduled Tribes in India*. Delhi: Isha Books (5 vols.).

Narang, Vaishna. 2008. 'Jero time: the Great Andamanese tribe and its perception of time', *Omertaa (Journal of Applied Anthropology)* 2008: 315–22.

Pande, Satish and Anvita Abbi. 2011. *Ethno-ornithology. Birds of the Great Andamanese: Names, classification and culture*. Pune: Ela Foundation, with Bombay Natural History Society and Oxford University Press.

Portman, Maurice V. 1887. *Manual of the Andamanese Languages*. London: W. H. Allen.

Portman, Maurice V. 1898. *Notes on the Languages of the South Andaman Group of Tribes*. Calcutta: Office of the Superintendent of Government Printing.

Portman, Maurice V. 1899. *A History of Our Relations with the Andamanese*. Calcutta: Office of the Superintendent of Government Printing (2 vols.).

Radcliffe-Brown, Alfred R. 1914. 'Notes on the languages of the Andaman Islands', *Anthropos* 9: 36–52.

Radcliffe-Brown, Alfred R. 1922. *The Andaman Islanders*. Cambridge: Cambridge University Press.

Radcliffe-Brown, Alfred R. 1933. *The Andaman Islanders*, 2nd ed. Cambridge: Cambridge University Press.

Raha, Manis K. 2005. 'The primitive tribes of Andaman and Nicobar Islands and their future'. In *Primitive Tribes in Contemporary India: Concept, ethnography and demography*, edited by Sarit K. Chaudhari and Sucheta S. Chaudhari, 11–28. New Delhi: Mittal (2 vols.).

Schmidt, Wilhelm. 1907. 'Die Sprachlaute und ihre Darstellung in einem allgemeinen linguistischen Alphabet', *Anthropos* 2: 282–329, 508–87, 822–97, 1058–105.

Shorto, Harry. 2006. *A Mon-Khmer Comparative Dictionary*. Edited by Paul Sidwell, Doug Cooper and Christian Bauer. Canberra: The Australian National University.

Som, Bidisha. 2006. 'A lexico-semantic study of the Great Andamanese: a thematic approach'. PhD dissertation, Jawaharlal Nehru University, New Delhi.

Sreenathan, M. 2001. *The Jarawas: Language and culture*. Calcutta: Anthropological Survey of India.

Temple, Richard C. 1903. *Census of India, 1901*. Vol. 3: *Andaman and Nicobar Islands: Report on the census*. Calcutta: Office of the Superintendent of Government Printing.

Yadav, Yogendra. 1985. 'Great Andamanese'. In *Papers in South-East Asian Linguistics no. 9: Language policy, language planning and sociolinguistics in South-East Asia*, edited by David Bradley, 185–214. Canberra: The Australian University Press.

Zamponi, Raoul and Bernard Comrie. 2020. *A Grammar of Akabea*. Oxford: Oxford University Press.

Index